Diary of a BRILLIANT KID

TOP SECRET guide to AWESOMENESS

~~pigeon~~ flamingo

yum

Shhhh, it's a cheat code to life!

Andy Cope, Gavin Oattes & Will Hussey

brought to life by Amy Bradley

CONTRACT

This book is different to other books. It has a contract. So, three things before you start: 1) read the small print, 2) have a go at the questions and 3) sign on the dotted line. No ifs. No buts. Only then are you allowed to read the book. Thank you.

SMALL PRINT: You must read this bit before you start even though the text is very small and annoying. We, the authors, do solemnly swear to write the best book we have ever written for the most important person in the whole wide world: YOU. We believe in you. We think you're amazing. We want you to have an epic life. But we can't do it for you. So, here's the deal: the book needs reading – like, cover to cover. No skipping the boring bits or 'speed reading'. It's a diary so there's some writing. The writing and drawing bits are important because they help the learning sink in. Plus, to be fair, most of them are great fun (especially the activity where you have to draw your own bottom). Failure to do the activities will make the learning null and void. And here's the best bit, if you actually soak up the content you will feel a shift in thinking and an upgrade of habits. Those habits will change your entire future.

But, be warned, there's effort involved in having a brilliant life. Most people can't be bothered. They kind of hope and expect that life will somehow unfurl, like some wonderful red carpet, and everything will be truly wonderful. It won't. Life doesn't work like that. We're here to provide the truth (and nothing but the truth) as well as a massive leg up to a life that really will turn out to be as dreamy as your bestest dream.

There are no guarantees, but this book will swing things in your favour.

Thank you for reading the small print. Sorry if it's made your eyes bleed. The rest of the text is much bigger.

This diary belongs to:

Age (to the nearest quarter):

If there was a fire and I could only rescue one thing from my house, that thing would be:

My ambition is to:

The best day of my life so far was when:

List at least eight reasons why you should love yourself: qualities, skills, good habits, good looks, etc. Don't worry, this is private so no one will see it.

1

2

3

4

5

6

7

8

Draw a suitable punishment for anyone who has stolen this diary and reads it. [Think slow, horrible death. Like eaten by baby wallabies, being made to drink gravy until they drown or the all-time classic 'death by donuts'.]

That'll teach ya!!!

HA ha!!!

YOUR SIGNATURE

___

Diary of a BRILLIANT KID

TOP SECRET guide to AWESOMENESS

Andy Cope, Gavin Oattes & Will Hussey

brought to life by Amy Bradley

This edition first published 2019

Registered office
John Wiley & Sons Ltd, The Atrium, Southern Gate, Chichester, West Sussex, PO19 8SQ, United Kingdom

For details of our global editorial offices, for customer services and for information about how to apply for permission to reuse the copyright material in this book please see our website at www.wiley.com.

Library of Congress Cataloging-in-Publication Data is available

A catalogue record for this book is available from the British Library.

ISBN 9780857087867 (pbk) ISBN 9780857087492 (ebk)
ISBN 9780857087881 (ebk)

10 9 8 7 6 5 4 3 2 1

Cover Design: Brought to life by Amy Bradley
Set in 14 pt Patrick Hand by Aptara
Printed in Great Britain by TJ International Ltd, Padstow, Cornwall, UK

DEDICATION:

To Karen (aka Amy's mum &
a real-life Mummy Bear, see page 55)

Thanks for everything you do
xxx

Also the world's
greatest baker
(washer + ironer!)

Stinky!

CHAPTER One: The End

In a nod to the fact that this isn't just 'any old book' we thought we'd start at the end. In fact, this chapter has a lot about 'endings': happy ones, not so happy ones, funny ones, Jessica's and yours.

It also has pancakes, ostriches and lion poo. Chapter 1 also has a terrific story which we're calling 'Gavin and the Caterpillar' that's well worth sticking around for. As is the most complicated sentence ever written.

It's a book like no other. It's the opposite of a book. A 'koob'? An *un*-book. I mean, the opening chapter contains the line *'blow a raspberry on learning's tummy'*. What does that even mean?

Confused?

Excellent.

Away we go…

Pancakes + Birthday ^yum^ Cakes

Let's rewind to when the world was pancake flat. It actually wasn't, but everyone *thought* it was, so fear of sailing off the edge meant that people stayed put. *'Don't sail too close to the horizon otherwise you'll fall off the end and die,'* kind of focuses the mind.

They didn't have cars, or school or YouTube. And they definitely didn't have Wi-Fi or iPads, otherwise they'd have been able to Google *'is the world actually flat?'* and chuckle at how silly they'd been.

Then someone found out the world was round. There was no edge to sail off, so away they went, sailing around the world, discovering new places like America, Australia and the Isle of Wight. If we fast forward to modern times, we've invented flushing toilets. We've learned to drive and Tweet (safety warning: not at the same time). And when you were born someone placed a smartphone in your chubby hand and you were like *'Oooogie. Blaaaah'* (it's an early version of *'#OMG!'*) and you started scrolling and swiping ... and dribbling on the screen.

You were born into a world that is new and different. Its super-fastness is super-exciting, and for the next 50 years your world is going to accelerate to super-duper fast. And then super-duper-pooper-scooper fast. Technology means we do things differently, which means we need to think differently.

The problem with human beings is that the world is pooper-scooper fast but our brains and bodies continue to evolve *slooooowly*.

This book will help you play catch-up. There's no doubt that school is important. Blow a raspberry on learning's tummy because it's so fab. All that reading, writing, science, Victorians, maths and stuff. Soak it up. It's useful. Enjoy it.

This book isn't about any of that.

We wanted to write something different. In big school you'll meet things called 'textbooks' – big, heavy beasties that make your shoulders ache as you carry them to and from school.

This book isn't one of those either.

In fact it's the opposite: an *un-textbook*?

Because one day you'll arrive at a job interview for your dream career. Like a scientist or a dentist or maybe a police officer or a jet-pack engineer. And do you know what they *won't* ask? They *won't* ask you any of these:

- Can you please tell me when the great fire of London was? Oh, and what street it started in?
- What's 6 x 7? And 4 x 8?
- How do you spell 'accommodation'?
- Can you make a papier-mâché Big Ben?[1]
- Any idea what an adjective is?

So, if that's exactly what they're *not* going to ask, what on earth will they want to know?

Here's your advance warning – to nail that dream job, they'll ask you to talk about yourself. What kind of person are you? What qualities do you possess? Give examples of when you've been stand-out epic and inspired yourself and those around you. When have you been a hero? How do you deal with a crisis (and please give examples from real life)?

Now, it helps if you also know about the great fire of London, and 6 x 7, and 'accommodation' and it's really cool if you just pull out some squidgy stuff and knock up a cheeky little papier-mâché Big Ben. They're the icing on the cake of success. But the cake itself is you.

[1] A note about footnotes. There will be several of these throughout the book. They give us an opportunity to say a bit more – an aside, so to speak – that is interesting, funny or informative. Except this one. This one was added because I was going to wonder, out loud, why papier-mâché is in French. Why do we have to use a French word for what is essentially glue and paper modelling? I was going to Google it, find out the answer and stick it in the footnote but I couldn't actually be bothered. So you've wasted your time reading this particular footnote, but all the rest are well worth looking at. Probably. Anyway, the footnote is finished now so back to where you left off please... which was 'Big Ben'.

Yes, in a sentence that's never been written in the English language before, you are a cake. A Battenberg, in fact (that's a yellow and pink one, which is especially yummy).

Our job is to turn you into the best cake you can be. That means you'll need some amazing ingredients in the right proportions, and to cook at the right temperature. Yes, we've taken this metaphor too far. Here it is in non-cake language: We are going to prep you for a dream job and epic life. The prep starts now. You can have your cake and eat it.

And here's how...

Continuing the cake theme, we want you to imagine something you've never imagined before – a large and steaming lion turd on top of a children's birthday cake. Please focus your imagination – the detail is important. It's a lovely cake and the lion poo on top is hot, fresh and stinky. It's spoiled the cake, to be fair. One more detail to imagine please – there are 43 children at the party, all aged 4. Let's assume it's Jessica's 4th birthday party. She's lovely btw.

Thank you.

Our point?

The lion poo is unpleasant in itself but also a warning of bad things to come. A lion at a children's party is rarely a good idea. It's not going to end well for Jessica. This book doesn't shirk the bad stuff. We're going to help you get big and strong in your thoughts as well as behaviours, so when bad stuff happens (which it most certainly will), you can deal with it.[2]

We're asking you to upgrade your thinking – to think differently from the rest of the population. It's almost cheating, but not quite. Because anyone can do it. It just takes a bit of practice and effort.

Here's an example of thinking differently. One of the authors of this book decided to study happy people. That's a pretty cool thing to do, and fairly simple, but nobody had actually done it before. All the scientists and

[2] Please note, the lion is used as an example. This book hasn't got anything that will help if an actual real lion turns up at the next party you go to. Maybe you can use the book to swat it while it chews on Jessica? But that's about it. Sorry.

doctors in the world, forever, had done the total opposite.

We've spent billions of hours and squillions of pounds studying unhappy people. Science has always been about finding out why unhappy/depressed people are feeling so low and then inventing pills to make them un-depressed. That's all well and good, but Andy decided to turn the science on its head. He had an idea ('ping', it came to him when he was making a papier-mâché Big Ben one day): what would happen if, for a change, we studied happy people?

So he did.

For 12 whole years.

He turned it into a job and became a scientist of it. Yes, an actual boffin of happiness. A Doctor of Joy.

So, normal doctors get people in to talk about their problems – *'So Mrs Winklebottom, tell me about all those*

times you were picked last for netball. How did it make you feel?' – and whoosh – Mrs W is transported back to when she was 9, feeling awkward and left out. And Mrs W feels bad all over again, aged 43.

Un-Doctor Andy's questions are more like *'Morning Mrs Winklebottom, that's a cool name btw, tell me about something brilliant that happened when you were 9,'* and the lady smiles and recalls all the times she did wonderful art and her teacher put her pictures on the wall. And she grins and feels *amaaaaaazing*, aged 43.

It's definitely *un*-therapy. And *un*-unhappy.

This simple switch in thinking is a bigger deal than it sounds. It's important because one of the things Andy found out is – get this – happy people aren't rich and famous. They don't have perfect lives. The sun doesn't always shine on them. They live in exactly the same world as everyone else. Sometimes they got picked last at netball too!

But they have different thinking.

That's basically it!

And this book is about that.

Thinking
they do this differently!

Andy calls them '2%ers' – the most positive 2% of the population. Two people out of every hundred. So when you see the phrase '2%ers', what we mean is the merry band of folk who have oodles of optimism, energy, happiness and positivity. We're going to reveal who they are, what they're doing to be a 2%er and, crucially, what we can all learn from them so that we can do what they're doing and live life as a 2%er.

2%ers. Positive folk. The ones who shine. We're gonna tell you how to be one.

Got it?

Good.

Let's crack on then.

Based on a True Story

You might be a big reader (someone who reads a lot of books, not a 7-foot-tall one). Or you might not be.

It doesn't matter. All that matters is that you read this book. We've gone to the trouble of designing it so it's very readable. It's got everything that a 'normal' book has – words, pictures, paragraphs, punctuation – everything, that is, except a story.

A book without a story? **Waddayamean**, it's not got a story? How can a book not have a story?

Just to confuse you, it has and it hasn't. It's not got a story as in '*boy wins ticket to chocolate factory and fat kid gets stuck in a tube along the way'*. Its story is YOU. Yes, YOU are the central character. The only character really. YOU are not only in it, but you are the glue that holds the story together.

Which is where things really hot up. We want your life to be an epic story of action, excitement, adventure and fun. We want it to be one of those fairy tales where you meet your perfect partner, fall in love (when you feel ready, obviously) and live happily ever after. You might have to kiss a few yukky frogs or live with seven dwarves somewhere along the way, but that's part of the adventure.

There's oodles of good news. Goodles. Your life story is up and running, and there are plenty of chapters left to write.

The not so good news is that everything is temporary. This book will end. And so will you. You will run out of days.

Just saying.

Ends can be sticky; like falling in to a vat of treacle, or super-gluing yourself to an elephant's bottom. You can also meet an end 'quickly', 'painlessly' or, indeed, 'spectacularly' – like inserting fireworks into places they were never intended for.

In fact, there are numerous ways to die, including:

1. Gargling with guinea pigs (which can also be unpleasant for said guinea pigs)

2. Ice skating without any ice

3. Forgetting to breathe

4. Climbing Mount Everest in shorts and tee shirt

5. Juggling with chainsaws.

So, just to re-iterate, this book will end, as will you. Which is probably all the more reason to enjoy the bits and pieces in between. You've a pretty decent chance of sticking around for the next 90 years, so there's really no point in worrying about the final chapter just yet.

The remaining 89 years and 364 days of 'not dying', however, are worth giving some consideration. Most people don't, and consequently they 'live' in a rather unspectacular manner; limping from one day to the next.

We wrote 'live' in inverted commas because it's important to know the difference between 'being alive' and 'living'. You see, technically speaking, you can be alive (showing all the classic signs: breathing, moving, eating toast, etc.) without really living. We figure that if you're going to the trouble of being alive, you should upgrade to '*properly* living'. It's more than having a pulse. It's about energy, passion, motivation, effort, colour, excitement.

Make that pulse race a bit.

'Not dying' is essentially counting your birthdays, but not enjoying the bits in between. It's really no way to live.

Here's the same thing in a different way: You have one birthday a year and 364 non-birthdays.

Ultimately, not enjoying the bits in between birthdays eventually leads to not enjoying the birthdays either. Which really doesn't leave much...

So, congrats, you're alive. But are you really living? And when you get a bit older and pressure really kicks in, will you be able to shine?

Word of the day

MEPHOBIA:

the fear of being so awesome that the human race can't handle it and everybody dies

Cool Rules 4 KIDS

Here are some rules. Don't question them. The rules are like gravity: you don't need to understand them, they just work.

Here goes...

We've written the rules to appeal to children, but big grown-up people will also benefit. So, if you get a moment, why not reverse the roles and YOU read a bedtime story to your mum, dad or gran?

Tuck them in. Sit on the edge of the bed. Open the book to this page and ask them, *'Are you tum-fur-cubble? Great, then let's begin...*

Whoop!!!

Rule One: You will receive a body

Whether you love it or hate it, it's yours for life, so accept it. Make the most of it and always remember what really counts is what's inside. This sounds like a bit of a cliché, but it's true. Eat good food (most of the time) and sleep well (always). Exercise your body every day. It's the only one you'll ever have.

Rule Two: Niceness and hard work together will always carry you farther than intelligence

Trust us on this one. Long term, it's true.

Rule Three: There are no mistakes, only lessons

Mmm, this is a tricky one because some things that you do will certainly feel like mistakes. You grow through a process of experimentation, so it's 100% guaranteed that things will not always go to plan or turn out how you'd want. Stop moaning. Who ever said that life was fair? Take the learning and move forward.

Rule Four: Be kind

Always. It's a happiness superpower and it's free.

Rule Five: Be grateful

Base your life on a bedrock of gratitude. Look at what you've already got and marvel at it, daily. Gratitude is like fertiliser for happiness.

Rule Six: Stand up for Mondays

Yes, a tricky rule to live by but one that's guaranteed to stand you out from the crowd. What if Mondays and Fridays are equal? They're both worth a 7th of your life. And you've accidentally learned to think like everyone else: they don't like Mondays so you've decided they're rubbish too.

So un-decide!

Mondays are epic. Celebrate Monday, just like you do Friday. Coming alive on Mondays is the coolest rule of them all.

Rule Seven: If you haven't got anything nice to say, then keep quiet

People sometimes say the wrong things. Most of the time they don't mean it. It's easy to be a troll. It's easy to be nasty, especially online. Don't. Ever. You will occasionally be on the receiving end of nastiness and trolls. They might be horrible people, or they might be nice people having a bad day. Either way, never retaliate. When they go low, you stay high. Kill them with your niceness.

Never post pictures of what you've had for your tea. Share worthwhile stuff. Be an encourager.

you AGAIN

Rule Eight: What you make of your life is up to you

100% true but very difficult to get across to young people without sounding like an old person (i.e., someone over 30). You have all the inner resources you need. You are bursting with potential. No pressure, but what you do with it is up to you. By age 23 there really is nobody else you can blame (that doesn't stop a lot of people trying).

Rule Nine: Stop trying to be the best in the world

And start trying to be the best FOR the world. You are in competition with one person and one person only – yourself. You are competing to be the best you can be. It boils down to this: are you a slightly better person than you were yesterday?

If you can answer 'YES' to that, pretty much every day, then you're growing.

Rule Ten: You will forget all this at birth

Doh! This 10th one is sooooo frustrating. All these cool rules and worldly wisdom. What a terrible shame you totally forgot it.

But you will. That's why you don't like Mondays!

So, can we add one more rule?

Rule Eleven: Be bothered!

TOTALLY.

There's a global shortage of positivity, enthusiasm, happiness and 'can-do' attitudes. 'Botheredness' is on the verge of being extinct.

It's more difficult to be positive than negative and, because it takes a tad of effort and a bit of practice, most people can't be bothered. Hence rule #11.

Remember, you've been reading these rules as a bedtime story for your mum. She might be snoring by now. Or she might be wide awake, hanging onto your every word. She'll probably want another chapter, but you've got to be firm. '*No mummy. That's it for tonight. You've got a busy day tomorrow so off to slumber mountain.*'

Kiss whomever it is on the forehead and back out of the room, '*Night night, love you, sweet dreams, mind the bugs don't bury into your skin and eat your flesh*', switching the light off but keeping the door ajar in case they get scared. Which, to be fair, they definitely will.

Now you've got time to reflect on the rules. Number 10 is a bummer, because it states that you'll forget them all. So that only really leaves number 11.

Get bothered. Know what? It's not a bad place to start.

BIG wisdom:

'Let others lead SMALL lives, BUT NOT you. Let others ARGUE over SMALL things, BUT NOT you. Let others Cry over SMALL hurts BUT NOT you. Let others leave their FUTURE in someone else's hands, BUT NOT you.'

Jim Rohn
(motivational American bloke)

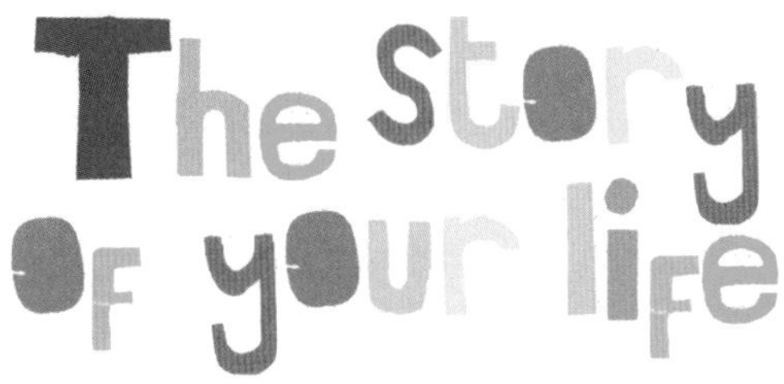

You are a story teller. Not just you, all humans are. Stories are what link us to our ancestors.

We have stories about everything. You started with cardboard books where 'A' was always for boring old 'Apple' and Z was guaranteed to be 'Zebra'.

Then you moved onto *The Gruffalo* and messed around with Horrid Henry. Before you knew it, you'd nailed Roald Dahl and now you're halfway through the Harry Potter series.

But you also have a story about you. Your inner story is one of the great classics, although only in your own head. Here's a cheeky little secret – you can tell a different and better story. In fact, changing your inner story is the fastest way to a better you.

Before we go any further, it's important that you understand something. It's a BIG 'something'. A 'something' that most adults don't get.

It's this...

Your happiness isn't real. Neither is confidence. Or sadness come to think of it.

The way you feel about yourself isn't real. It's all

self-generated, created by the story you tell yourself. This happens silently, inside your head. There's a technical word for it – *thinking!*

We're going to hammer this point later, but it's worth thinking about now so you can be thinking about your thinking before we come back to thinking about re-thinking how you think about your thinking. *Eh?*[3]

But, of course, you're the author of the story of your life. You might not be able to change the events that have happened, but you can re-cast yourself as the hero. That changes how you view the past and, spookily, will affect how you approach the future.

So let's fast forward, not to the end of your life, but to age 71¾...

ACTIVITY: LOCAL HERO

Imagine you are 71 years old and you've achieved some AMAZING things in your community. A bit of a local hero, in fact. Your local newspaper (which might be online) is writing an article about you.

What would you like the headline to be?

(in 8 words or fewer)

[3] Read this sentence to the person next to you. See if, between you, you can make sense of it.

Write the story (what have you achieved, what personal battles have you won, what have you made happen in your life, what are people saying about you, what quote would you give the newspaper reporter; the reporter has tracked your teacher down – what would they say about you?)

"I wish I was a glow worm,
a glow worm's never glum,
Cos how can you be grumpy,
when the sun shines out
your bum."

The Glow Worm Song

Shine O'clock

This book is based on a true story.

Yours!

But we also have ours. This is Gav's...

When I started training as a primary school teacher I still felt like a child. I had just turned 18 and had never really been out of school. Like most people, I went to nursery, then primary, secondary, university and then right back into primary schools. My life had gone full circle.

I'll never forget my first ever day as a student primary school teacher. I arrived in a school where the head teacher can only be described as a SCARY WEE WOMAN. Sounds like a terrible Super Villain. Imagine the movie title, Wonder Woman Vs Scary Wee Woman![4]

I made my way into the staffroom; I felt like I had made it. I was nervous as I had never been in a staffroom before. In the middle of the room was a table with chocolate biscuits on it. Not just two or three biscuits but hundreds of biscuits, maybe thousands. Millions even.

[4] If your teacher is reading this to you and your head teacher is proper scary, turn and look at your friend beside you and give them a nod.

You might not know this, but this is why children are not allowed in the staffroom: because of the biscuits. You'll eat them, and the teachers want them, so they don't let you in. Ask your teachers. They'll deny it, but it's true. Staffrooms all over the world are basically chocolate biscuit factories. In fact, some of the tables and chairs are carved out of chocolate biscuits. Behind the door your teachers stuff their faces with chocolate biscuits and you're not welcome.

Imagine Willy Wonka's Chocolate Factory with rivers of chocolate and giant gummy bears.

That!

On my first day, I sat staring at the biscuits. I tried to count them but I couldn't. I lost count after 1,892,465 and a half. A lady approached me, *'Are you Gavin?'* she asked. *'The student teacher?'*

I had so many biscuits in my mouth that when I turned to say hello about 23 biscuits flew out of my mouth and landed on her face. She had a chocolate finger up her nose. But I hadn't been eating chocolate fingers.

'Yes, I'm Gavin.'

She pulled the chocolate finger out of her nose and ate it. (I'm not sure if this part is true or if I made it up, but I hope it is.) *'You're with me,'* she said, *'in the nursery.'*

NURSERY? The nerves well and truly kicked in; I nearly had another little accident! I was terrified. Nurseries are just big rooms full of 3 and 4 year olds, mini Oompah Loompas, running and eating. They eat when they're running and run while they're eating. Even when they're not running and eating, in their minds they're running and eating.

The teacher turned to me and told me that she would like me to pick a book and read it to the class. I did a double take. *What? I thought I was here to observe. Me? Reading a story? To 40 Oompah Loompas?*

My heart raced as she herded the tiny human beings into the reading corner. *Gulp! My first test!* On the top shelf was my favourite book of all time, *The Very Hungry Caterpillar*. I realised this was my big chance to win the kids over.

I sat on the big chair, you know the one.

The children were sitting wide-eyed and waiting. Legs crossed, except for the ones who couldn't. You might be one of those ones; the ones who can't cross their legs. But we're still made to cross our legs. I am one of those ones. You might be too. I used to have to snap my legs into place.

Every child sat and looked at me with their best face – do it now for me please, so you can remember the face I'm talking about – a mix of anticipation, love, Christmas Eve and awe. If you're reading this book in class, tap the person next to you on the shoulder and show them your 'best face'. Your '4-year-old-about-to-be-read-a-story-to face'.

I don't think these kids had ever seen a male teacher before.

I took a deep breath and began to read the book. After the first couple of pages I thought I'd have a quick look up just to make sure the kids were okay. As I lifted my head I realised something strange had happened. Every single child appeared to have moved closer.

I carried on reading. Another couple of pages and again I looked up; every single child was even closer. Or were they? Was I imagining things or were they carpet ninjas?

I decided to try and catch them out. I looked down but immediately looked back up again. I caught them! Every single one of them on their bums moving forward like a wee army of ants – they were killer ants, coming to attack me.

Keep reading the book, keep reading the book, I told myself.

One tiny boy began to take my shoe off.

Keep reading the book, keep reading the book.

I could see my shoe being passed all the way to the back of the class.

Keep reading the book, keep reading the book.

I could see my shoe being passed along the back row. One little boy was flying my shoe, the next was chatting into it like a phone and one even licked my shoe.

WHY? Why would you lick a shoe? All I could think was *keep reading the book, keep reading the book*, that's what I had been asked to do. *'On Thursday he ate through 4 strawberries, but he was stiiiill hungry...'*

My shoe was now on its way back. From the corner of my eye, I could see it being passed forward from child to child. It finally reached the front row, made its way back to the same child who removed it in the first place and, like a professional shoe fitter, he simply popped my shoe back onto my foot, checked the toes and loudly stated for all to hear, *'I'VE GOT TWO SHOES!'*

I learned in that moment exactly what happens when a 4 year old publicly announces how many shoes he/she has.

EVERYONE publicly announces how many shoes they have! And guess what? All 40 of them also have two shoes!

All of a sudden, amidst the global announcement of how many shoes everyone was wearing, things moved up a gear. Another small child began to climb my leg. Now, when I say 'climb', I mean climbing, actual climbing. I'm certain this kid was wearing a rucksack and carried a map. And a compass (I'm not sure if this part is true or if I made it up, but I hope it is).

So, picture the scene: I'm now sitting in front of the whole class and there's a small boy sitting on my leg just staring at my face. I tried to ignore him; I'm a professional, right? But we were almost nose-to-nose. So I turned and said, *'Can I help you?'*

'I just really wanna see the pictures,' he replied.

'Have a quick look at the pictures and then get off my leg!' Before I could even finish my sentence, I began to feel a very warm sensation appearing on my leg. Now, in this moment my mind began to race. A few things could've been happening, but I could only think of three.

1. I'm being peed on

2. I'm being pooed on

3. This kid is naturally a very warm child.

I was praying for number 3. I have a feeling as you read this you are willing it to be number 2.

[Number 2... funny... see what I did there?]

I asked him, *'Are you naturally a very warm child?'*

Nothing.

'Are you weeing on my leg?'

To which he simply smiled and began to nod.

Note, all our stories have a point. None are silly. Not even the silly ones.

Remember your 'best face' – the one Gav asked you to pull halfway through the story about the story? That's you at your best. It's you in 'interested mode'. It's the wide-eyed, oh-my-gosh-I-can't-wait-for-whatever's-coming-next face. Scientists call it 'flow' – the version of you that is totally absorbed in life, where time passes quickly and everything seems easy.

You did 'that face' a lot when you were 4 and, if you're honest, those wide-eyed moments are tailing off. You still have moments of excitement, where life is a roller-coaster ride, but the gaps between them are getting longer. Being so engaged with life that you can't sit still – that's worth aiming for. Inching forward towards adventure – that's a wonderful feeling. Enjoying the roller-coaster thrill of life – that's a good way to be.

Obviously, if you get so excited about life that you wet yourself, then you've taken things too far.[5]

[5] **TECHNICAL NOTE:** that might happen a few times when you're in your 90s and some body parts aren't working so well.

Quote that's wiser than it sounds:

SO much time, and SO little to do!

Strike that, reverse it.

Willy Wonka.

The End.
For real this time

You might need to sit down for this one. Oh, and there are no laughs at all. Quite the opposite in fact.

There's a saying: you only live once. And it's 100% incorrect. You only *die* once. You live every single day.

A doctor decided to ask her patients what they enjoyed in life, and what gave it meaning. All well and good, except this doctor happened to work with terminally ill children. 'Terminal' is just the worst word. In an airport, a terminal is where your journey ends. In a hospital, that journey is life. These children don't get better. Ever. They're not going to get to enjoy the pleasure of being an adult.

Here are some of the children's responses.

First: none said they wished they'd watched more TV; zero said they wished they'd spent more time on Facebook; zilch said they enjoyed fighting with others and not one of them enjoyed hospital.

Interestingly, lots mentioned their pets and almost all mentioned their parents, often expressing worry or concern such as, *'I hope mum will be OK. She seems sad,'* and *'Dad mustn't worry. He'll see me again one day in heaven maybe.'*

All of them loved ice-cream. *Fact!* Also, they all loved

books or being told stories, especially by their parents.

Many wished they had spent less time worrying about what others thought of them, and valued people who just treated them 'normally'. For example, *'My real friends didn't care when my hair fell out.'*

Many of them loved swimming, and the beach. Almost all of them valued kindness above most other virtues: *'Jonno gave me half his sandwich when I didn't eat mine. That was nice,'* and *'I like it when that kind nurse is here. She's gentle. She doesn't rush. And it hurts less.'*

All of them loved people who made them laugh: *'The boy in the next bed farted! Hahaha!'* [Laughter relieves pain.]

And finally, they ALL valued time with their family. Nothing was more important. *'Mum and dad are the best!' 'My sister always hugs me tight' 'No one loves me like mummy loves me!'*

Look here, dear reader, these are very big messages indeed. If you can't be bothered to listen to anything else in this book, then please listen to children who are arriving at the final destination of their very short lives.

If we were allowed to summarise, it'd be something like this: Be kind. Read more books. Spend time with your family. Crack jokes. Fart in bed. Go to the beach. Hug your dog.

Oh... and eat ice-cream.

Often.

Stiff Gum + 1p 2p Small Change

Putting your hand down the side of the settee can be a sticky business; you never know what you might find. In fact, in terms of places you might consider putting your hand down, it's probably best avoided (along with 'your pants', of course.)

It's quite possible, however, that should you feel the urge, you might retrieve one or more of the following items:

An old, stiffened piece of chewing-gum (covered in assorted hair)

a broken biro

a selection of coins.

Firstly, even though you'll be tempted to recycle the gum, it's best not to. You know from experience . . .

Secondly, it's estimated that down the side of the nation's sofas lurks a small fortune – something to the tune of £155 million is lost each year. We're guessing not all of it was found down the side of the *same* settee. That would be just careless.

But small change, it seems, is worth something.

This book is not really about settees, stiff gum or even 10-pence pieces. But it is about the value of small changes, and how thinking about things in a different way might make, err… a BIG difference. And not just for you – but for those you share the settee with, and anyone else, come to think of it. So, who are those people?

People I share the settee with:

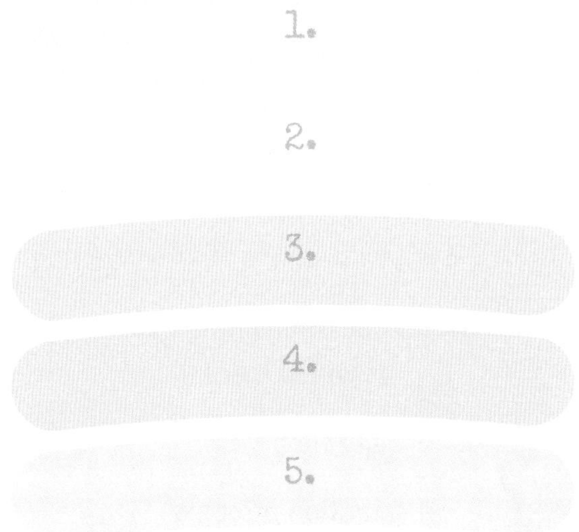

This book is about you but it's much bigger than that. If you get 'you' right, the people on your settee will also feel amazing.

If you're under the age of 12, it's quite possible that your future career hasn't even been invented yet. Just let that sink in for a moment; it's exciting and a tad scary at the same time.

A bit like sushi.

Teachers, shelf-stackers and hairdressers will probably still exist in some form, but so will a whole host of futuristic other ways to make a living. You might, for instance, become:

a second-hand jet-pack sales guru

a Botox removal engineer

or a trainee digital quark wrangler
(whatever that might be).

It's not something you need to get worked up about; after all – tomorrow will still be there when you get around to it, or rather when the world turns around to it. It does suggest, however, that between now and then, some things will have to change.

Or, to put it another way – very few things will stay the same. And yet the vast majority of us like 'the same'. In terms of footwear, 'same', would be a pair of old slippers: warm, comfortable and reassuringly familiar (if a bit smelly). We wake up and get dragged out of bed (or not) the same time every Monday morning. You probably enjoy the same pizza for tea every Thursday (most likely pepperoni).

We fall into regular routines of doing what we do, because that's what we've always done. We're creatures of habit, but if change is inevitable, then maybe it's worth being prepared for it. Maybe we could even welcome it. Maybe we could even change for the better. That's right, even you.

Do you know this person…

“As a child, Zaphod had been diagnosed with ADHDDAAADHD (ntm) ABT which stood for Always Dreaming His Dopey Days Away, Also Attention Deficit Hyperflatulance Disorder (not to mention) A Bit Thick.”

Douglas Adams, The Hitchhiker's Guide to the Galaxy

BONUS ACTIVITY:

The 'School Reunion'

Reunion
20 whole years later!

Twenty years from now you are going to meet up with everyone in your class for a night of catching up, reflection and sharing what you have achieved in your life.

How old will you be in 20 years?

[Good, well done, although to be fair, adding 2 lots of 10 to whatever age you are now isn't that hard].

Now imagine that you are that age. Write two pages that reflect on your 20 years. Here are your instructions:

Page 1: Imagine you've coasted for 20 years. You dossed around at school and wasted your time. Basically, you couldn't really be bothered, neither at primary or secondary. Your attitude has been questionable. Your dog ate an awful lot of homework. Your grades were iffy. Your teachers were frustrated.

Write about how your life has turned out. What job are you doing? Who are you with? What do you own? How do you feel? What do people say about you?

Page 2: Imagine you've been awesome for 20 years. You knuckled down at school and had a superb attitude. Your dog helped you with your homework. Your grades were magnifique and your teachers purred with pride.

How has your life turned out? What job are you doing? Who are you with? What do you own? How do you feel? What do people say about you?

Compare your potential lives.[6] Which do you fancy, future 1 or future 2? They're both available to you.

The killer point from the two futures you have just written about is that future 2 requires more effort.

Yes, the dreaded 'e' word.

You have choices. You can choose easy. You can stop reading this book right now and aim for the rather rubbish future #1 – the lemon-squeezy, low-effort option.

But if you've got this far we think you'll read on. You're intrigued to know the secrets of a stellar future. You're going to choose effort. In which case you're in the running for awesomeness.

Quit waiting. Step forward. You can raise the bar or you can wait for others to raise it.

Adopt the brace position (nothing to do with teeth) because, either way, in Chapter 2 that bar is getting raised!

[6] We'd like to read these. 'Brilliant' tee-shirts for the best ones.

CHAPTER TWO:

How to be a Flamingo in a Flock of Pigeons

Firstly, try saying *'Flamingo in a Flock of Pigeons'* 10 times as fast as you can.

Secondly, welcome to Chapter 2, a collection of our most epic writing that's got levels, like a computer game. With levels! You'll love our re-telling of Goldilocks and our story about radiators. Then, in a chapter about 'Flamingos and Pigeons', we go all goosey and set some spine-tingling graveyard homework.

We'll tell you how to be a squillionaire. Scrub that – we'll tell you *why you're already a squillionaire* and we'll chuck in a chance to be the 4th best in the world. We encourage you to sniff a donkey. In October if you can. While eating Haribos.

But that's bonkers, so we'll start softly softly, with a story about Gav's brush with the law. It's true . . .

The POLICE Incident

Have you ever considered the lack of imagination in who discovered the first ever orange? Marvelling at this special spherical fruit, they must have tasted it and gone, *'Wow! But what should I call it?'*

I guess we should be thankful that whoever discovered the banana had a bit more imagination, otherwise you'd have been opening your lunchbox and peeling a 'yellow'.

That aside, settle in for a rip-roaring story that involves oranges, the police and hanging. And, guess what, it's TRUE!

Gav is loaded; he's made a fortune from selling 24-carat-gold toilet seats. He wanted to send something to his loyal customers that was a bit different from the usual letter or email; something that would (eventually) lead to the loo. A free gift that would make the gold-panners go wowza. Not only different but healthy, bright, surprising, colourful, juicy, full of energy and with a big dose of zing. Something you wouldn't expect to receive from the postie. Something that would put the biggest of smiles on people's faces.

'It's obvious,' exclaimed Gav at his Monday morning

meeting. *'Oranges. We'll send oranges in the post. Five hundred of them. Half a thousand big, juicy, ripe, bright orange oranges.'*

'But that's ridiculous, no one sends oranges in the post,' piped up his less-enthusiastic colleague.

'Egg -zactly!'

So, a plan was formed. Gav went to the supermarket and bought every single orange they had. Still 106 short, he drove to the next supermarket and bought theirs as well. Gavs-ville was literally orangeless. It was starting to develop scurvy.

Lovingly, each orange was individually gift-wrapped, followed by a trip to the post office to dispatch 500 spherical bundles of zesty glee. The very next day, all Gav's wonderful customers would receive a gift of health, colour and zing that would keep them all 'regular'. They'd open the orange-shaped parcel to find a small sticker on the orange with a link to the website. Simple.

What could possibly go wrong?

The very next morning, 500 gift-wrapped oranges landed in the receptions of schools, colleges and businesses with golden lavatories across Scotland. Gav was beyond excited!

Then the phone began to ring. This was it; the first customer to have received an orange. Surely they were calling to say how much they loved the unique approach and that they wished to order more toilet seats?

Gav smiled as he lifted the phone and put it to his ear.

'HOW DARE YOU DO SOMETHING SO STUPID! WHO DO YOU THINK YOU ARE, SENDING AN ORANGE TO A SCHOOL? ARE YOU AN IDIOT? DO YOU REALISE WHAT YOU'VE DONE?'

'Sorry, what did you just say?' gulped Gav, the smile rapidly disappearing.

'PUT ME ON TO WHOEVER CAME UP WITH THIS FRUIT-BASED, HAIR-BRAINED SCHEME.'

'That'll be me, Sir,' spluttered Gav.

'ARE YOU SOME KIND OF MORON? YOUR COMPANY HAD BETTER NOT CONTACT US EVER AGAIN! AND BY "EVER", I ACTUALLY MEAN "NEVER EVER"!'

'Sorry, err... who is this?'

'THIS IS Mr McHEADTEACHER OF McMISERY HIGH SCHOOL AND I HAVE ALREADY SPOKEN TO THE POLICE ABOUT THE MCMESS YOU'VE CAUSED! DON'T BE SURPRISED IF THEY TURN UP AT YOUR DOOR.'

Gav was sweating. A lot. *'Why would the police be turning up at my door Mr McHeadteacher?'*

'BECAUSE YOU SENT ME AN ORANGE! WHO IN THEIR RIGHT MIND WOULD BE SO STUPID? I HAD TO EVACUATE THE ENTIRE SCHOOL!'

'Why?'

'BECAUSE I THOUGHT IT WAS A BOMB.'

'Pardon? You thought what?'

PHONE WENT DEAD

Almost immediately there was a knock at the door. *'Open up, it's the police.'*

The door opened to reveal three cops. They did not look happy. *'We're looking for a world-famous author. A Mr Gavin Oattes.'*

Gulp! *'That's me,'* spluttered Gav. *'Err... come in.'*

'Mr Oattes, it has come to our attention that you've been sending oranges in the post.'

'Erm. Yes.'

It's a weird thing and you probably won't realise until you get a bit older, but whenever you meet a police officer, you immediately feel guilty. Gav held out his hands, waiting to be cuffed. *'... Five hundred. Gift-wrapped. To schools, mostly.'*

'Why Mr Oattes? Why on earth have you been sending oranges to all the schools in Scotland?'

'We wanted to send something that would, err... get people talking...' Gav's voice trailed off.

The policeman raised an eyebrow.

'Have I done something wrong officers?' whispered Gav, feeling guilty, but not knowing what of.

There was what can only be described as a pregnant pause. Not quite the full 9 months, but it felt like it. Maybe there was an olde-worlde law that Gav didn't know about, from 1284, that deemed sending oranges through the post as something punishable by Sellotaping your eyes open and dripping vitamin C into them.

The pregnancy ended and the policeman gave birth to his next sentence. *'No, actually it's not an offence Mr Oattes, in fact, it's quite a clever idea. Thanks for your time Mr Oattes,'* the policeman grinned.

'Would you like some oranges to take away with you?'

'Aye that'd be great, thanks. And could you also sign my book?'[7] And with that, the policeman was transformed into a please-man.

So why share this story?

Two things really. Firstly, try not to cause bomb alerts. They're never a great idea. Secondly, and most importantly, never be afraid to stand out. Be you, post

[7] Okay, that bit didn't actually happen. But the rest of it did. More or less.

oranges, be different, be brave. No matter how hard you try in life, there will always be 'them'. Them who just don't get it, who don't get you, who just don't see the world the way you do. Be glad that you're not one of them.

We'll be returning to this theme later. For now, all you need to know is that the world has a confusing message. On the one hand, you're encouraged to be yourself: *'Just be you. Go for it! Stop caring what other people think.'*

So then you do that, and the world says, *'Oh! You're not fitting in. You're a weirdo. You need to conform.'*

'Fitting in' is okay. Human beings are wired to fit in and act normally. We think that's fine in the short term – say if you're sitting on a crowded bus. But your best long-term strategy is to dare to stand out. Getting noticed for the right reasons means you have to show up, step up and do things better than you have to. Not only will other people look at you positively, but you'll come to see yourself as someone who has an important part to play: a main character.

Remember, you don't have to do what everyone else is doing. Follow your own direction and you'll soon be leading the conga.

Gav's next campaign... *Watermelons!*

Even the cops said it was awesome.

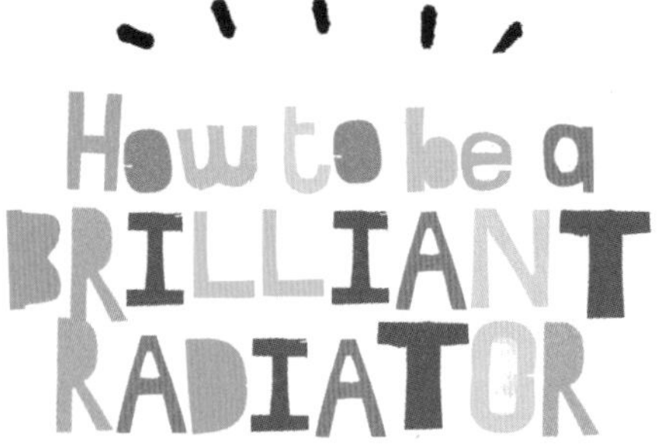
How to be a
BRILLIANT
RADIATOR

Next level.

As household heating appliances go, the radiator knows it all. It's a silent, wall-hugging witness to the daily to-ings and fro-ings of family life; it watches, ever-present, through night and day, come rain or snow.

Compared to other central heating components, a radiator has surely got one of the plum jobs. The toilet, for instance, has to put up with a lot of, err . . . poo, and only gets to see the inside of the bathroom (or the 'downstairs cloakroom' if you live in a posh house).

That said, there are radiators and there are radiators. Whilst you're probably now sorely tempted to go lean against a wall for three or four hours, throwing some rectangular shapes, we'd like to suggest another way.

Radiators, you see, give stuff; 'warmth', usually. Some people manage to do that too. But not all. Some folk radiate the opposite, and this book's not about them. We're back in 2%er territory: the special ones; the few; the givers; the best of the best; the radiators. The people who not only give off warmth, but also love, happiness, positivity and confidence.

Have you noticed something? They make you feel amazing.

So maybe it's time to out them. The wonderful people in your life who, when they're around, you feel kind of uplifted, happy, positive, confident, warm.

Here's your challenge. It's a three-parter and it requires you to be a little bit braver for each part:

Part 1: Make a list of the 2%ers (really positive people who make you feel amazing) in your life. AND, not only who they are but what it is that they do that makes you feel amazing.

Name of positive person:	What they do that makes me feel amaZZZZZING

Part 2: of the challenge - pick one of the people off your list - someone who has helped you in life, or inspired you, or looks after you and loves you unconditionally. Write them a thank-you letter. Tell them what they've done for you and how grateful you are.

Part 3: Read the letter to them. **TODAY.** Now if you can. In the space below, tell us what happened when you read it:

How you make others feel about themselves says a lot about you. So, be a radiator. And definitely, at all costs, avoid being a drain. Or a hoover; they suck.

mmm porridge

Goldilocks + the Free Bear

Goldilocks was having a lie-in. She's 14 after all. That's what happens.

Baby Bear had been ages in the bathroom trying to clean himself up. It was true what they said about bears; the poo really does stick to your fur. Anyway, he did his best, flushed the toilet and went downstairs. Baby Bear plonked himself in his small chair and looked into his bowl. It was empty. *'Who's been eating my porridge?'* he squeaked.

Daddy Bear arrived at the big table, stretched, wiped the sleep from his eyes and plonked himself in his big chair. He looked into his big bowl and it was also empty. *'Who's been eating my porridge?'* he roared.

Mummy Bear poked her head through the serving hatch from the kitchen and yelled, *'For Goodness' sake, how many times do I have to go through this with you idiots? It was Mummy Bear who got up first. It was Mummy Bear who woke everyone in the house. It was Mummy Bear who put the kettle on. It was Mummy Bear who unloaded the dishwasher from last night and put everything away. It was Mummy Bear who swept the floor in the kitchen. It was Mummy Bear who walked the dog. It was Mummy Bear who set the table.'*

Mummy Bear was like – well, a bear. With a sore head.

Baby Bear's bottom lip was trembling, but she continued, *'It was Mummy Bear who cleaned the guinea pigs out, gave them their food and refilled their water. And now that you've decided to drag your sorry bear-backsides downstairs and grace Mummy Bear with your bear-faced cheek, listen carefully, because I'm only going to say this once...*

'I HAVEN'T HAD TIME TO MAKE THE PORRIDGE YET!'

We love the modern telling of this traditional story. There are loads of great points, especially that even brilliant people are allowed to get a bit angry sometimes. Let's look at what being brilliant isn't. Being 'brilliant' *isn't* about always being right or nicey-nicey. And it's certainly not about being walked all over. It's not about sticking a stupid grin on your chops and pretending to be happy when you're seriously hacked off. Sometimes it's perfectly OK to be angry and upset.

Just not all the time!

And, hopefully, if this message has sunk in with all you baby bears out there, wouldn't it be great to help out a bit more, or occasionally to make the family bears' porridge? Or give ma bear a big bear hug and tell her she's the best Mummy Bear in the whole world, evs. Ditto for pa, grandma, big sis and Aunty Brenda bear.

It's most definitely a good thing to be the opposite of selfish. Which is probably 'otherish'. Being otherish means being willing to give more than you receive, but still keeping your own interests in sight. Being kind, considerate and ultra-helpful – these are habits that you can easily adopt.

Your life isn't just about you. It's about how you positively impact on the lives around you.

Be a giver, not a taker.

ACTIVITY: EXTRA-ordinary

We're going to give you three simple statements. Without over-thinking them, scribble the answers in the spaces below. Truthful answers please.

Be the kind of learner your teacher wants you to be, which is...

Three things I will do to make my teacher go 'WOW':

1

2

3

Three things I will do, today, that will make my family go 'WOW':

1

2

3

Channelling Your Inner Goose

Next level.

Did you know that we humans can learn loads of incredible stuff from geese? Yes, that's right, geese! Take a 'gander' below... (Gander? Anyone? As you were.)

Goose fact 1, geese are really tasty. If you've never tried goose, trust us, it's like chicken. But more... *goosey.*

Goose fact 2, a collective group of geese is commonly known as a gaggle BUT only when they are on land. In the air they are known as a skein, team or, our particular favourite, a wedge of geese. If you ever see a wedge of geese, you'll notice they fly in a V-formation.

Goose fact 3, if you want to be the best human you can possibly be, then you need to learn to channel your inner goose.

Confused? Good; limber up those wings, shine those beaks and prepare to get honking.

Before we learn 'the way of the goose', here's a quick and very true story involving 40,000 superheroes all heading in the same direction.

Fairly recently, one third of your writing team – Gav –

figured that he'd run a marathon, as you do. Have you ever watched someone run a marathon? It's a crazy undertaking that requires months of training, and anyone who decides to run one is clearly some kind of machine, or goose, or both. Part machine, part goose: Robo-Goose? Gav thought that if he was going to commit to this then he might as well run the most famous marathon in the world. A trip to London beckoned.

Gav claims the London Marathon is, to this day, one of the most fun, uplifting and inspiring experiences of his entire life; which is weird considering the fact that a) all his toenails fell off (let's all just think about this for a second… BARF!), and b) he didn't even win (in fact, a giant SpongeBob sprinted past him on the final 100 metres and he was beaten by a tyrannosaurus rex).

What's this got to do with geese? Keep reading.

Gav was pounding the pavement with 40,000 people, each and every one running for a reason; a positive reason. Running with a purpose. Whether that was to win, set a new PB, to have fun, to raise money for a charity, to raise awareness of something meaningful, remember a loved one or to support a loved one, everyone was running in the same direction (apart from the guy who ran backwards. Although, technically he was still moving in the same direction).

Gav's only competition that day was himself. The other runners played their role in keeping him going. Runners were encouraging each other, helping, supporting, stopping to check on those struggling in the heat and some literally carrying complete strangers over the finish line. At about 16 miles Gav spotted a spectator holding what looked like a fishing rod. Hanging on the end was a horn, one of those proper old-fashioned horns that you have to honk properly. Attached was a sign that read 'Free Honks to Keep You Going', and boy did Gav honk that horn. And yes, it kept him going; it made him smile and his energy lifted yet again.

Gav was channelling his inner goose.

This is the very reason geese honk: to encourage others to stick together and keep on going. How cool is that? Our Gav basically turned into a goose during his marathon. Well, not really, but it's still cool, right?

When a goose falls ill, is wounded or shot down, two geese drop out of formation and follow it down to help and protect it. How amazing is that? Would you stop and help a friend or classmate who needed your help? The geese stay with the injured goose until it is able to fly again or until it dies. Then they launch out with another formation or catch up with the flock.

And as if geese weren't already awesome enough, let's take a closer look at that V-formation. As each goose flaps its wings, it creates an 'uplift' for the birds that follow. In other words, by flying in a V-shape, the whole flock makes it easier for the geese to stay up in the air.

This adds a greater flying range of over 70% than if the bird flew alone.

When the lead goose tires, it rotates back into the formation and another goose flies to what's called the Point Position. It's tougher at the front, so they take it in turns. They are always looking out for each other, helping, supporting and encouraging.

And this was the big London Marathon takeaway for Gav (in addition to the fish and chips he had afterwards) – it seemed that at every moment he began to slow, struggle or hurt – and he assures us there were many (remember, he started with 10 toenails and ended with none) – there was someone or something in place to lift his spirits. It all came from people and their kindness, their humour, their creativity and energy.

Everyone needs free honks to keep them going from time to time. Be an encourager. Be a goose, a pal, a superhero, a Robo-Goose, look out for others, be there, create 'uplift', stick together, lead from the front when it's your turn. You'll go 70% further. And when others need it, HONK as loud as you can.

Acts of Kindness
ACTIVITY

Being kind doesn't have to cost anything. It's a bonza way to live your life. When you're kind to someone, that makes them feel like a 'somebody' and it makes you feel amazing too.

EVERYBODY WINS.

So, go out of your way to be extra kind. List 10 things you'll do THIS WEEK that will make someone's day:

Homework that goes BUMP in the night

This book is crammed with big grown-up stuff. Yes, we've cunningly disguised it so you hardly realise, but trust us, there's BIG content throughout. But none BIGGER than this. You might need to go and get changed into your swimming cozzie before you read this next bit. Goggles on? Adjust your budgie smugglers, because we're going into the deep end...

Your thinking is designed to fool you. Not just you, of course, the whole of the human race. We've all fallen for it. You're tricked into thinking that 'I am me' in this body in this time called 'life'. And your feelings are created by things that happen to you.

Once you fall into this particular thinking trap, you begin to chase 'things' that will make you happy. You equate 'success' with 'how much stuff you can buy' or whether your phone is better than your mate's. You have succeeded so long as you have loads of stuff.

Some goose-bumping homework

Find your local graveyard and have a wander. Probably not at night, deffo not if there's thunder and lightning, and if you see a headless horseman, our top tip is to run. *Fast!*

If you pick a sunny Saturday, you'll be fine. Have a read of the tombstones. Most will be from a long time ago, so they'll have funny names like Agnes or Horace (in exactly the same way that in 200 years people will be chuckling at gravestones with 'Annabelle' and 'Harry' on) but it's less about the names and more about the comments.

I challenge you to find one that says *'Here lies Dave. And he was really cool because he had a Lamborghini'*, or *'Dear departed Mary. She was epic cos she was minted'* or *'In memory of our dearest mother, Kylie, who will be remembered forevs for her really epic selfies and she had so many pairs of shoes it was like totally unreal'.*

Challenge

The tombstones in your local churchyard will tell a very different story.

Who wants to be a Squillionaire?

You want to be rich? (Call it a lucky guess.)

There's a strong chance that you already have riches beyond your wildest dreams. One of the London universities has worked this out:

- Having good friends and relatives is worth £64,000 a year to you
- Having nice neighbours is worth £37,000 a year
- Have a waggy dog? £36, 448 (and 16 pence) of happiness every year (cats are much less and pet anteaters scored zero)[8]
- And the biggy: excellent health is estimated to be worth £300,000 a year to you.

We sincerely hope you can tick some of the boxes above. So here's another very big point. We take the things above for granted. We fail to spot them and our attention is focused on all the stuff we haven't got.

Taking the argument to the extreme, I guess you could trade in your family, friends, neighbours, good health, cat and anteater and collect about £400,000. And we're sure you'd be nearly half a million pounds richer, but

[8] YES, we made the pet one up. It's most probably true but we can't prove it. The other ones are facts.

so much poorer. There are so many ways to feel good. Some of mine are fitness, fresh air, clean pants, foreign lands, today, fulfilment, kindness, accomplishment, bacon, hugging my children, Netflix, misty mornings, very hot curries, having my cat on my knee (while watching Netflix; this is a double whammy. If I'm eating bacon at the same time then I'm off the scale of wowza), the smell of a donkey, Haribos and October.

And yours? What are your feel-good factors?

Going for GOLD

Have you ever met anyone who can honestly say they are the 4th best in the world at something?

What about 4th best beard in the world? Nevermind this 1st, 2nd or 3rd best beard nonsense, 4th best beard is where it's at.

A few years ago our very own Gav entered the World Moustache and Beard Championships. Yes, it's true, this is actually a thing that exists. Men (and occasionally women) from all over the world spend years growing, shaping, taming, sculpting and moulding their facial whiskers and every two years they gather somewhere in the world to celebrate the best of the best.

Gav only found out by chance about the World Moustache and Beard Championships, 90 days before the actual competition, and decided to enter. But there was a problem: he didn't have a moustache or a beard.

So, without any egging on from anyone, Gav filled in the forms and the growing began. He entered a category called 'Partial Beard Freestyle'. Again, this is actually a thing.

He had a simple three-pronged attack strategy:

- No shaving for 90 days
- Style it the night before the competition
- WIN!

For 90 days, slowly but surely Gav's beard began to take on a life of its own and, before he knew it, it looked like a giant loaf of wholemeal bread had invaded his chops. Crumbs! People laughed, others pointed. Occasionally Gav was met with shouts of *'Hey Chewbacca'*, *'hairy face'* and his particular favourite, *'How many birds live in there?'*.

Games of *'How Many Things Can You Hide in Gav's Beard?'* became a regular fixture. And just in case anyone is wondering… 17 is the record.

Here's the thing, people would poke fun at Gav's ever-growing facial forest of fuzz. Gav, however, kept on growing.

The 90 days dragged **ON** …

• • •

On the eve of the World Moustache and Beard Championships, Gav drove for 9 hours and, in line with the original plan, in his hotel, Gav styled his beard.

The initial plan had been to style his beard into the word 'BEARD' but Gav was concerned that because he was doing it in the mirror, the result may, in fact, read 'DRAEB' or 'BREAD' or 'DAFFODIL'.

So a last-minute change of plan resulted in an epic sweeping moustache/sideburn combo with an enormous chin-talon of awesomeness. Gav nodded approval to the freak in the mirror, donned his kilt and headed off to represent Scotland in the most prestigious moustache and beard competition in the world.

When Gav turned up he couldn't believe how many other contestants there were. Over 300 beard growers from all over the world had arrived. Beards down to the floor, spikey beards, curly beards, even beards in the shape of London Bridge; every single style, shape, size you could imagine and more.

Over the next three hours, a strange combo of London Fashion Week and Crufts for humans proceeded to unfold; 2000 people turned up to watch. Yes, 2000 people left their homes to look at beards and moustaches.

Gav's name was called and he took to the stage, his facial

masterpiece receiving thunderous applause.

He came 4th in the world.

You will rarely meet anyone else in life who has achieved such a thing. Throughout this story you have probably been wondering why on earth Gav or anyone else would have given the time and energy to such a bizarre undertaking.

It's simple.

Because he can.

It may be a bit different from the norm, but hey, normal is boring, right? It might be a bit weird, but hey, weird is exciting, right?

It's no different to why people play football, sing, dance, draw, build and so on. Because they can.

You don't even have to be the best, but you can still be a part of something. You can still compete. You can still have fun.

It's amazing when you find something that's your thing. Something you can get into and be bothered about.

Who knows, you might even come 4th in the entire world.

CHAPTER Three: Eat. Move. Sleep. (FLUSH)

There's something about Chapter 3. We can't quite put our fingers on it. Maybe it's the cleverest chapter, or the least clever; the funniest, or the least funny.

It starts with superheroes and ends in superheroes. It's got chimps and a trip to the zoo.

There's mind-blowing science and a drawing activity that's so cool it'll make your bottom squirm. We're aiming to re-think your thinking and tip you into ninja-thinking mode.

Then we move to food, explaining why you love fast food and hate veggies. Oh, and there's a terribly sad story about a bear called 'Beatriz'.

And in recognition of getting this far, look out for a world first – we're going to give you £200,000. It's a free gift! Just like that. Yours for the taking. £200,000! If you're reading this in class, nudge the person next to you and whisper, *'Oh my goshness. I'm about to get nearly a quarter of a million quid.'*

Hiss it loudly, so even your teacher hears.

Ker-ching!

Strap yourself in and away we go . . .

Optimus-Rhino

On Gav's first day at school he was asked to stand up in assembly in front of the whole school and share what he wanted to be when he was older. Three other children stood up alongside Gav. Oh, and remember, he's from Scotland.

Child 1: *'When I grow up I wanny be a hairdresser.'*

Child 2: *'I wanny be a train driver.'*

Child 3: *'When I'm older I'm ganny be a fuutballer.'*

Gav: *'When I'm bigger I wanny be a rhinoceros.'*

Gav is now bigger and, guess what, he's not a rhinoceros. Not because he can't be one, but because he's 'changed his mind'.

Did you know you can be whatever you want in life?

Well, OK. Let's be really open and honest here. You can't always be *exactly* what you want to be. Gav can't really be a rhinoceros for one simple reason: it's impossible. Gav's a human, apparently. Gav may argue that it's because he changed his mind. And if you ask Gav what he changed his mind to, he'll tell you: Optimus Prime.

He can't be Optimus Prime either.

But he *could* work with rhinoceroses, or he *could* design transformers for a living, right?

If you think about it, there's always a way. This is because we're human beings and we're absolutely awesome. We're born awesome, all of us.

Did you know you're born with invisible kneecaps? They literally don't show up in x-rays even though babies definitely do have kneecaps! This is awesome.

Did you know you were built for genius? Actual genius.

I bet some of you reading this are thinking, *'Nope, not me, not a chance, there's no way I'm a genius.'*

Likewise, one or two of you might be thinking, *'Of course. I knew that. Because I'm a genius.'*

You have one hundred billion brain cells that make ten thousand connections each at any one time. Do you know what having one hundred billion brain cells allows you to do? Anything.

Well, almost anything.

It allows you to produce enough saliva in your lifetime to fill two swimming pools. How cool is that?

Your brain is amazing. And just like your Intergluteal Cleft (Google it…), it's especially amazing when you use it.

There's one particular part of your awesome brain we want to draw your attention to. It's the part that turns you into a superhero. It gives you superpowers.

It's called your imagination. You'll have heard loads about it before, but do you really know what it's capable of? It's time to use your imagination…

You might just think it allows you to think about stuff differently, but did you know your imagination and thoughts create your future? Think about how awesome that makes you; you can see the future!

It's all too easy to get stuck in life and feel like we're not moving forward, but our imaginations allow us to focus on the real life that we want to experience. Your imagination allows you to take the 'everyday' and turn it into something magical. Again, it's your superpower.

Think back to when you were 4 years old and someone handed you a cardboard box. What did you do with it?

Drove it. Flew it. Decorated it. Sailed it. Transformed it. Surfed it. Ate it.

You turned it into anything you wanted.

With your imagination.

Think about this for a moment. With just your imagination you turned a regular cardboard box into a submarine.

Again, awesome.

We bet you're smiling as you're reading this. Taking a moment to remember what it was like to view the world through the eyes of a 4 year old reminds us of the joy and wonder that imagination brings.

So let's test our imaginations right now.

We want you to write a letter to yourself from the 4-year-old you, offering you some advice for life. Just what would a 4 year old have to say? Go on, give it a bash. This exercise is done best sitting cross-legged with crayons in one hand and Hula Hoops on your fingers. The carton of Ribena is optional.

Letter to myself, from the 4-year-old me.

Dear older version of me, here are my **TOP TIPs** for a fabulous life...

Give a chimp a banana
and it will eat the banana

Give a chimp a lot of bananas
and it will share them

Give a chimp a a room full of bananas
and it will kill other
chimps to protect them

No, we're not quite sure what
that means either. But it's true.

Chimp-an-See

Going bananas

Look at yourself in the mirror. Now I don't want to get too deep too quickly, but have you ever stopped to consider which bit is 'you'?

Is it the body bit? Grab your ear lobe and feel the smoothness of it. That's a bit of 'you', right? Or bite your lip. Ouch, that's definitely 'you'. Punch yourself in the face. *Thwack.* [editor's note: this is getting ridiculous, please stop asking children to harm themselves]

[authors' note: but we're having such great fun]

Our point? There's a physical 'you'. That version of 'you' that's basically a bunch of trillions of cells stuck together. It's the one you can slap. And the physical 'you' is very important.

But this chapter is less about the 'you' that you see in the mirror. Yes, yes, we know you're gorgeous but herein lies the clue to you #2. Who's the one noticing your reflection? Who's the one saying, *'Crikey your hair's so wonderful today'* or *'doesn't my bum look amazing in these knickerbockers?'* Who's the one imagining what kind of day you might have today?

We reckon this is the real you. The lumpy, visible bunch

of cells is just the mechanism you use to transport yourself around. The one in your head is the most important. The one that feels and connects. Some call it your spirit or inner chimp. It's actually your thinking.

What messes most people up is the view inside their head of how life's supposed to be!

Your inner voice is often full of negative chatter. It's self-critical. It's your *'I can't do it', 'I'm not clever enough', 'What will people think of me?', 'I'll never be as good as so-and-so'* voice.

Just in case you were wondering, everyone has that voice. We'd like you to start noticing the voice and challenging it. In a nice way. In fact, we're challenging you to upgrade to a better inner voice for the next two weeks. To upgrade your thinking, it might be useful to think of your negative inner voice going away for a couple of weeks. So, pack its suitcase and send your negative inner voice on holiday or, better still, if it's an annoying chimp, send it away to the zoo, leaving you free to be the brilliant version of yourself.

What a fabulous opportunity! While the slightly rubbish version of you is swinging on the tyres or throwing poo at the public, the brilliant version will be shining at school and home.

Enjoy inhabiting the brilliant version of you 24/7. Smile more, laugh a lot, shine in class, try your very best, thank your teachers, be kind, help out at home, do your homework without grumbling (and do it superbly so your teacher goes 'wow!'), say nice things about people behind their back, walk tall, be confident, raise your hand in class, have a go, role-model positivity …

If it doesn't work out, you can always revert to the rubbish version of you. But we're pretty sure that after two weeks of being amazing you'll want to keep your negative inner voice where it belongs, safely behind bars.

In a nutshell, here's what you'll have learned by the time you're 50: most of the bad things you worry about will never happen. Most of the bad things that do happen will have never crossed your worried mind.

Cool! Now you don't have to wait till 50 to stop worrying!

Imagine you are 119 years old and have one minute left before you die. Your great-great grandchild is holding your hand and asks, 'Before you die, tell me what should I do with my life?'

Write your advice:

Grey matter matters

Concentrate now. Here's the science bit.

Your brain weighs about as much as a bag of sugar. If you're a baby, it'll be less, unless you're actually reading this at the age of three months old, which will mean your brain is amazingly well-developed. A fully-grown adult's brain will weigh a bit more – even in the ones that are a bit dim. Unless you're a scarecrow – in which case you've probably got a turnip instead.

Brains are not always something that we give much thought to; 'out of sight, out of mind', as it were. Which is strange, really, as your brain *is* your mind. You don't pay too much attention to your brain, mostly due to the fact that it's quietly nestled away in the cupboard under the stairs, known as your skull. The only time you pay your brain any real attention is when it drum-rolls on the insides of your bonce and generally causes a bit of a headache.

Yet your brain is the most powerful super-computer known to human kind (we think). It is capable of all sorts of weird and wonderful crazy stuff, and it does most of it on auto-pilot: sleeping, breathing, swallowing, digesting. But there's more to being amazing than just eating and sleeping. (Unless you're a sloth. Or a teenager.)

Spending your life on auto-pilot has its time and its place – usually when you're in bed asleep. But when you're awake, it's definitely wise to switch to manual. Otherwise you end up sleep-walking through your days, which is not really living.

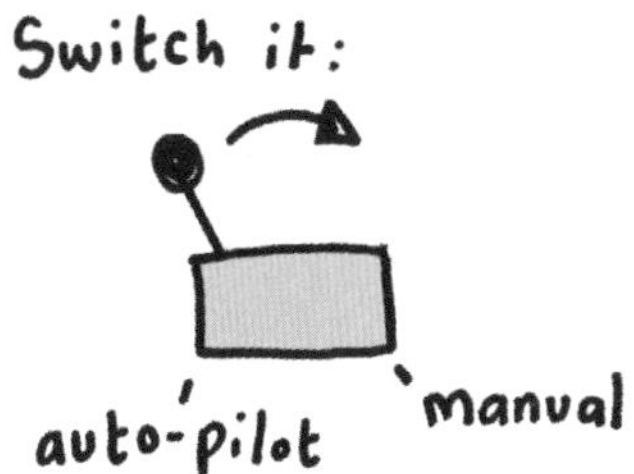

Auto-pilot just won't do it. Following others probably won't get you where you want to be. Doing nothing won't achieve anything, apart from obesity. Choosing to do the right thing, because it looks and feels like the right thing to you, will change your world for the better, and the worlds of everyone you happen to come into contact with. Cool, eh?

BODILY art

Here's a stunning activity. We know you're gonna love it...

Draw your bum when it's wandering around your kitchen or walking home from school. Yes, we know, it doesn't walk home on its own. It's attached. Draw your bum when it's having an active day.

Now draw your bum when it's been sat on all day. Literally, aaaallllllllll day. One of those days where there's lots of sitting in class and an assembly where you sit on the floor, and then you sit down for your tea and sit down to watch YouTube. It's like the one above but squidged and flat. Probably.

Draw your brain when it's alive. When it's thinking, alert, happy and full of life.

Now draw your brain when it's half asleep. When it's bored and can't be bothered. A TURNIP-BRAIN.

And now the easy one. Your face. Let's do the happy, excited, energised face first...

And now draw the miserable one. The bored, bad attitude, negative, 'life's so unfair' one...

The faces are easy. Because you can look around and see happy and sad faces. Faces are on the outside. But did you know that what's on the outside affects what's on the inside? The sad face produces a sad brain, droopy shoulders, rubbish chemicals invade your innards and your bottom goes saggy (maybe). When you wear a sad face your energy actually leaks away.

The happy face? Well, if you reverse the things above, you'll be pretty much spot on. The outside affects the inside. Plus, one other vital point – a smile makes you more gorgeous!

#NoBrainer

It's easy to get stuck in grumble-mode and, yes, it can be tough being a young person in the modern world, but not as tough as being a baby eagle. They learn to fly by being pushed out of the nest. Imagine. Mum gives them a nudge and yikes, they have 500 feet to learn!

Slow learner? *'Hmm… maybe if I try giving this a fla…' SPLAT!*

Your brain is the most complex thing in the universe, so let's dumb it down using 'old' and 'new'. The old part of your brain doesn't think, it just reacts. It dates back a few million years and is rather like a lizard's brain; exactly, in fact. And, boy, is it quick. The old part acts faster than you can think. Put your hand in a fire and you'll see what I mean – there's no *'Hmm, is that sausages for tea?'* – the old part of your brain acts at supersonic speed. Hand is withdrawn. And no; don't try it.

A few hundred thousand years ago, humans developed a new part of the brain, the neo-cortex; that's the bit above your eyebrows. This serves two incredibly useful purposes: firstly, it allows you to keep your hat on and, secondly, it's your thinking brain. This relatively new bolt-on is what distinguishes us from, say, crocodiles (that and the fact their scaly skin is perfect for handbags and shoes. Oh, and their jagged teeth and a few other bits and knobbly bobs).

This new bit is slower than the old part, but it allows humans to think, ponder, imagine, reflect, sulk and worry. Crocodiles don't worry ... about anything. Think about it, have you ever seen a crocodile actually shedding crocodile tears?

This new bit of brain is wonderful, but there's a design fault. It's programmed to spot danger and to worry about what might happen. For example, your *great great great great great great great great great great* grandpa (squared) could make two kinds of mistakes: First, thinking there was a snake in the bushes when there wasn't one, and second, thinking there was no snake in the bushes when there actually was one. The cost of the first mistake was a pounding heart and needless worry. The cost of the second one was death. So your brain is designed to make the first mistake a million times to avoid making the second one even once.

Read that bit again so it sinks in. It's actually rather cool.

Cut to today and the dangers aren't there anymore, but we have the same brain wiring – continually scanning for danger. This is just the way it is. It's not just you, it's the human race. It's called 'negativity bias' and it's always lurking in the background.

That means you have to re-train your brain to notice the positives.

So here's a really cool tried and tested activity that will help you tune into positivity and, crucially, it will gradually reshape your brain and begin to tilt it towards happiness and gratitude.

Three good things ACTIVITY:

Ask your teacher if the class can all have a go at this. For the next week we want you to write down three good things that have happened, or three good things that you've noticed. It's best done at bedtime.

They don't have to be massive events, but we want you to take two minutes at the end of each day to make a few notes. For example, they can be events, such as *'I put my hand up in class today and got an answer right'* or simple moments like *'I noticed the lovely blue sky today'*.

Record the activity and the feeling in the spaces below:

good things:

Day 1:

good things:

Day 2:

1

2

3

good things:

Day 3:

1

2

3

good things:

Day 4:

1

2

3

MY feelings:

MY feelings:

MY feelings:

MY feelings:

good things:

Day 5:

good things:

Day 6:

1

2

3

good things:

Day 7:

1

2

3

Extra
extra
extra:

MY feelings:

MY feelings:

MY feelings:

Ninja level

Here are a couple of biggies. The first is to realise that everything you ever feel comes from your thinking. Note, most adults don't know this. They assume that their feelings stem from what's going on around them. So it's work that's making them grumpy, or the queue at the supermarket that's making them tut, or one of the kids in your class that's irritating your teacher.

When, actually, you cannot have a feeling without a thought. So it's not work, the queue or the kid, it's the way they're *thinking* about them that's causing their feelings. There are no exceptions to this rule. Not a single one, ever. Go on, have a go at proving us wrong.

Think of the last time you felt any or all of these feelings: happy, grumpy, moody, jealous, annoyed, positive, stupid, embarrassed, excited, lonely, loved, crazy, like eating cake, sad, confident.

Let's take happy as an example. You might say, *the last time I felt happy was on Saturday morning when I woke up and realised it was Saturday. No school! Yippee!*

And we'd say it's not 'Saturday' or 'no school' that's making you feel happy, it's the way you're *thinking* about 'Saturday' or 'no school'.

Let's pick another: embarrassment. '*The last time I felt embarrassed was when I put my hand up to answer a question and got it wrong.*'

Again, nope, it's not getting the question wrong that's causing you to feel embarrassed, it's the way you're *thinking* about that situation. If you change the way you think about it, you'll get a different feeling. So, for example, you could feel *proud* that you put your hand up and gave it a go when everyone else had bottled it. Or *brave.*

It takes a bit of getting your head around, but once your bonce is around it, you get a calmer and more positive life. Everything you ever feel is just thinking. So change your thinking and, hey presto, you get a different feeling.

Have a go at a few.
We'll kick you off with an example...

Example of a strong feeling:

Monday morning; not wanting to get out of bed

What was the situation:

It was Monday! Need I say more?

What was I thinking at that time:

Everyone knows Mondays are a bit drab

Changed thinking:

I am not 'everyone else'. I am me! Monday is another opportunity to shine

All-new shiny brill feeling:

Hooray! It's Monday!

Example of a strong feeling:

What was the situation:

What was I thinking at that time:

Changed thinking:

All-new shiny brill feeling:

Example of a strong feeling:

What was the situation:

What was I thinking at that time:

Changed thinking:

All-new shiny brill feeling:

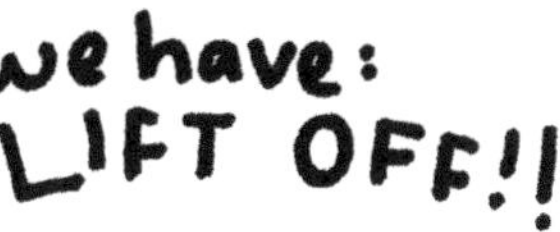

Hopefully the penny will have started to drop. It's not the situation. It's not what's actually happening around you, it's how you're thinking about it. That's where your feelings come from. No exceptions. Ever.

Once you 'get' that all your feelings are coming from your thinking (and nowhere else, ever) you have a couple of options. The first is to realise that it's just thinking. Once you realise that you have about 80,000 thoughts a day, you can let the negative ones pass and wait a millisecond for the next one. If it's a happier, more positive thought, jump aboard and it'll get you out of your grump.

In the book that keeps giving, here's another science gem. When a rocket launches, it uses 90% of its fuel to get off the ground. So there's a massive effort in getting started. Once it's done the first half mile, things get easier and once it's in space, it shoots forward almost effortlessly.

Hang onto your pants, if you realise it's just your thinking, you have lift-off . . .

One of our fave brain cheats is learning to change your language. We all face problems, challenges, things to overcome, hurdles, setbacks, difficulties, complications.

Whenever they crop up (which they will, often), start calling them 'plot twists'.

So when something doesn't go according to plan, it's not a nightmare, or unfair or the end of the world, it's merely a plot twist.

Shout it out. Rejoice! All good stories have a plot twist, an unexpected turn of events that nobody saw coming. Some books have several. Remember, your life is a story; a true one! Plot twists are inevitable. They're there to make things more interesting.

Plot twists! *Woo Hoo*. They exist because you're alive. Without them, everything would feel a bit – straight.

We're not sure what's above ninja level. Grandmaster ninja? Blackbelt? Robo-Ninja? Ginger ninja? Ninja biscuit?

Whatever it's called, this is it. Read again

Have you ever asked yourself, what hasn't happened that I didn't want that I haven't celebrated? Feel free to read that line again. And again. And again.

Sadly, unless you're a black belt happiness ninja, your mind doesn't sit in a maths lesson thinking how lucky you are to have a nice school and a wonderful teacher. It curses because you have to remember stuff. When you're on your games console and your mum shouts that it's tea time, you don't rejoice that you're going to get your tummy filled with yummy grub, you curse because you want to finish your level. On Monday morning when your dad tells you it's time to get up, you don't leap out of bed rejoicing that you have a house, a family and school chums – you disappear under your warm duvet and curse at your misfortune (that's a whinge-a-ninja).

The opposite of savouring good experiences is to notice the many things that could have gone badly, but didn't. We'll ask again, in a brain-twisting way – what *hasn't* happened that you *didn't* want that you *haven't* celebrated?

Here's my list for today (and it's only 7am): I woke up and didn't have toothache. My laptop isn't broken. I haven't got measles. My children aren't poorly. I haven't just stubbed my toe, we haven't run out of Cheerios, there hasn't been an earthquake and I haven't been bitten by a zombie.

I mean, what a fabulous start to the day. None of those bad things have happened!

Of course, it's hard to notice something that *didn't* happen. But it's helpful sometimes to switch your thinking to all the bad things that could have happened, but didn't. And then celebrate the positive result.

Have a go, it's fabulous fun. In fact, it's one of those mental muscles that gets stronger the more you exercise it. We'll get you warmed up, and then you can write your own list of bad stuff that hasn't happened that you haven't celebrated.

Here are your starters... the accident you didn't have, the power cut that never happened, the headache you didn't suffer, your kidneys that didn't stop working, the rain that never came...

...over to you – what hasn't happened that you didn't want that you haven't celebrated?

– bad stuff that's absent from your life.

1

2

3

4

5

6

7

8

9

10

Mood hoovers

they suck!

Some people are grumbly and negative. We call them mood hoovers – they're not horrible people, just stuck in a way of thinking that sucks all the happiness and energy out of themselves and other people.

Energy vampires.

Them.

It can be quite a challenge to maintain your positive approach to life when you're surrounded by mood hoovers. But if you apply the previous lesson, you'll twig that it's a bit weird, but nobody can make you feel anything. Sure, it may look that way, but if someone says something nasty, you can only feel sad/angry/irritated/miserable/upset by having a thought about what they've said. Thought gives birth to feelings. But thoughts come and go. They flow by. A massive river of thoughts, one after the other, forever. You can't ever stop the flow. It's impossible to stop thinking, but you can choose some sparklingly brilliant thoughts.

Try it. Try and think of nothing. Or try not to think of a toddler wearing a tutu dancing with a bear that's wearing pink dungarees. Or, here's an interesting one: what would happen if we told you it was impossible to lick your elbow?

Exactly! You're trying to do it right now. Thoughts are going to keep coming at you. There are so many thoughts flowing by that you can't choose them all. But here's how it works: the thoughts that you choose, well, they turn into your feelings.

We all get frustrated by other people. You might be really good friends with someone, but then they get angry at you for some reason, or they behave without consideration, and all of a sudden, your mood is much darker. You're not happy with them; maybe they're not happy with you. Things can go sour very quickly.

This is such a difficult problem that there is an entire library of books devoted to ways of working out these kinds of frustrations. But we have one technique that, if applied consistently, will lead to a lot more happiness.

The secret: always think the best of other people.

↖ A life changing TIP.

Allow us to explain by taking the opposite view first, the mean-spirited one. Let's say that, for some reason, you've been left out of an activity, game or party. It's easy to see the rudeness, inconsideration and plain wrongness of other people. You have no idea why they would be so mean; you're a good person who doesn't deserve that. These are natural reactions, but looking at things this way only causes you to feel bad about the other person. You are frustrated, angry, offended or hurt. You build up resentment. You might also react badly to the other person – say something hurtful or angry, ignore them, or whatever. So you're not happy and neither are they. This isn't a good situation.

The best-of view is a better way to live your life. It takes a bit of practice but when someone does something inconsiderate – and we're not saying their actions are justified – you can try to think of those actions in a good-hearted way. For example, maybe they're having a bad day and are in a grump. That doesn't excuse their actions, but you can understand the feeling of being grumpy.

Now't as funny as folk

People are so unpredictable. I'm constantly amazed at how different my twin daughters are. Abi is so much more positive and confident than her sister, Hog Face.

The best-of approach tries to see the good in the other person, to assume that they are nice people with good intentions who make mistakes and are having trouble of some kind. In short, they're only human. For example, they didn't realise you'd be upset, or maybe they're just having a bad day. This is not an excuse for bad behaviour, but you can understand it, because sometimes you accidentally do it too. Yes – even you.

We said this can be difficult, but please hang in there. Once you see them in a positive light, you react better. You stay calm, you forgive, you remain upbeat and you manage to smile through it. Being nice to someone you dislike doesn't mean you're fake. It means you're mature enough to control your emotions.

The next time you feel difficulty with someone, try the best-of view. You just might find some happiness in a difficult situation. And besides, life is too short to spend time with people who suck the happiness out of you.

We've got some good news and bad news for you. First of all, the bad news. It's this: *the news.*

And now the good news. Well, there's loads but you won't see it on the news.

Confused? Let's explain. Whatever it is, if it's brand new, straight-out-of-the-box, packaged to perfection, and – best of all – shiny, it feels... good.

Things that feel good new:

Phones. Most new phones are not actually 'new'. Usually, they've had several years of languishing in the bottom of your mum's handbag, or resting next to your dad's bottom. Your mobile phone is typically new to you, with a sprinkling of fluff. So not new at all.

1. Toilet Roll. Enough said. Don't touch the nearly-new stuff.

2. Shoes. New shoes always look great, even if they don't always feel great. School shoes tend to look good until you meet up with your friends. Then you question just why you count them as friends, after your shoes don't look quite so new anymore.

3. Haircuts. Haircuts can look and feel amazing, or they can make you want to hide. A good haircut has superhuman qualities; making you feel as though you can single-handedly take on the world. A bad haircut (a 'scarecut') is like having a tattoo of your parents kissing. You literally daren't leave the house.

4. Puppies. New puppies are adorable until you actually get one. Then, very quickly, whatever appeal they once had is negated by scrubbing a succession of small 'accidents' off the front room carpet with your little brother's toothbrush. Your little brother gets a nasty shock before bedtime, too.

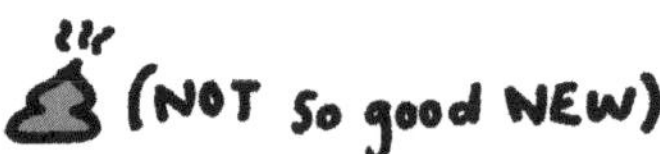

So, not all new stuff is good new stuff. Sometimes, it can actually be quite unpleasant.

It's wise to recognise the difference between 'new stuff', and 'news tough', they're not the same.

News is supposed to be new, although it can feel like the same things go wrong again and again. It's like recycling, but in a bad way. The news is nearly always bad, the worst of the worst: the biggest earthquakes, the hottest forest fires, the bloodiest wars, the scariest criminals, the worst car crashes, the windiest winds...

It's true that, from time to time, stuff does go pear-shaped; sometimes in a big way. And we're not here to pretend otherwise. But we are here, like a camera, to: a) shed a little light on things, and b) put them into perspective.

Only tough news makes the news. Good news – the complete, beautiful, heart-warming opposite – very rarely does. And the reason it doesn't make it on to the news bulletin is because, well... if it did, there simply wouldn't be time for anything else.

Every day, all around you, in every single country of this beautiful planet that we have come to know as Earth, men, women and children do monumentally marvellous things. They help, befriend, love, give, build, care, share and shine, just – well... just because.

And if the news included all the good news, there simply

wouldn't be room for anything else in the schedule – all day, every day. Which seems quite a cool thought, really.

So, we can't pretend that bad stuff doesn't happen, but in comparison to all of the good stuff, it's but a tiny poo in a magnificent flower garden. We'd rather it wasn't there, of course, and it makes sense to try and avoid putting your foot in it, but the garden is still a beautiful place, nonetheless.

Beware of the news. It's half an hour of talking about the dog turd and zero minutes talking about the garden.

A Thoroughly Modern Muffet

Little Miss Muffet
Sat on a tuffet
Eating her sarnie from Greggs.
Along came a spider
who sat down beside her

So Miss Muffet took a picture
and posted it on social media

Too much ing-ing

Back in olden times, there were no supermarkets. You couldn't just wander to the shop, pick what you wanted, and scoff it on the way to school. Food was scarce and there were no taps to drink clean water from. Fatty food gave our ancestors extra reserves of calories to call on during the times when food ran out. Salt helped them retain water and avoid dehydration. Sugar helped determine whether berries were edible or poisonous. Fat, salt and sugar – they helped keep our ancestors alive.

Old habits die hard! The world has changed but we still crave those naughty foods. We're basically wired to love fast food.

Stick your listening head on and get a load of this. Fact: heart disease (not in a good way) is the number one killer in western Europe and yet there's a tribe in Africa that never die from heart disease. The Hazdas from Tanzania also have the healthiest guts on the planet. So we travelled to northern Tanzania to find out what we could learn from the Hazdas…

Brace yourself for a new kind of diet – the berry and porcupine. Yes, you read it correctly. It's all about microbes, you see. The Hazdas super-wellness starts off inside their guts. The nomadic nature of Hazdas means they don't have possessions, or fridges, or shops. Yes, in another sentence that's never been written before, the Hazdas have no Asda. On a daily basis they eat what they can catch, or what's on the bushes. Hence, a balanced mixture of berries and porcupines; some grubs too, apparently. *Yummy!*

Which brings us to another rather big 'so what'? Are you really suggesting that I, the reader, accompany my mum to Asda and look for the porcupine section? Or that we forage in the park for nuts and berries?

Gosh no, our point is soooo much bigger than that.

The basic structure of human beings is hunter-gatherer. Not that long ago, and with the Hazdas it's still the case, life was active. You were born on the move. Nowadays we're living in classrooms, or in front of screens, scrolling, texting, emoji-ing, selfie-ing, swiping. We're ing-ing.

Hunting information and gathering social media likes, and sugar. That's created a mismatch between how your body is designed and the world it's designed for.

Next time you're in the supermarket (when your family's doing the big shop, not the little shop) take time out to notice how food is sold to us.

All the unhealthy food shouts loudly. Have you noticed that the ADHD food behaves as if it's actually got ADHD? Take a walk down the wild aisle. The sugary cereals are screaming that they've got 30% reduced sugar or they've been pepped with added vitamins. *'Look at us. We're fortified!'* They're shaking their fists and bulging their biceps as you pass by. *'We'll show you how to start your day… on a sugary high.'*

Now wander down the veg aisle. The carrots? Totally quiet. Apples? Not a murmur. Lettuce? Think about it. Have you ever seen a TV advert for lettuce? Imagine an excited voice-over man shouting *'It's green and crispy. It's crammed with goodness. Lettuce. Have it for your breakfast or as a tasty snack at supper time'* – cut to a smiley child chomping on some green stuff. Caption: *'Iceberg lettuce. So tasty it can sink an ocean liner.'*

Nope. Lettuce sits on the shelf like a Trappist monk: a deafening vow of silence.

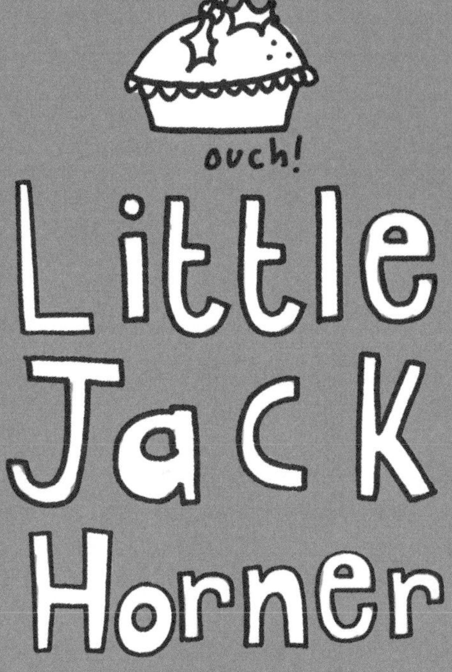

Little Jack Horner
Sat in the corner,
Eating a Christmas pie;
He put in his thumb,
And burnt it.

But we've not told you the whole story. There's a problem with the Hazdas, you see. With such healthy microbes, you'd think the Hazdas would live forever, but no. The reason they *never* die from heart disease is the same as why they haven't ever had a case of Alzheimer's – because they never live long enough, what with lions, snakes and packs of wild dogs.

Berries and porcupines? On balance, our advice is to stick to Asda. But the healthy aisle.

Here are our modern-day DOs and DON'Ts for eating properly, having energy and living forever...

- DO sit down and eat as a family (as often as possible). If it's not happening, insist that it does.

- DO switch off the TV and phones. Chat. Ask your family what the highlight of their day has been.

- DO appreciate your food. That means savouring it and thanking whomever provided it. That might be God but, more likely, Tesco Extra.

- DO add a bit more porcupine to your diet (but careful of the prickly bits, they tend to get stuck in your throat).

- DON'T eat in front of a screen or standing up.

- DON'T eat without cutlery or out of a box.

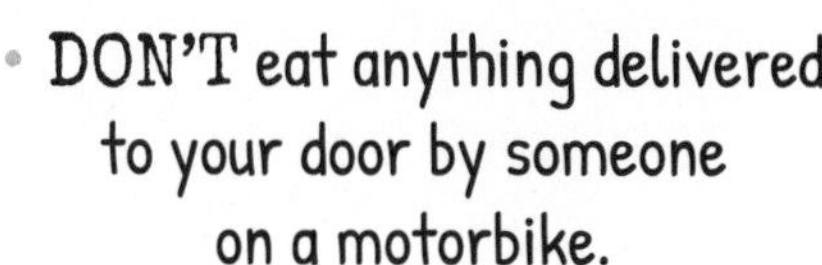

- DON'T eat anything delivered to your door by someone on a motorbike.

- DON'T eat anything passed to you in your car through a hatch.

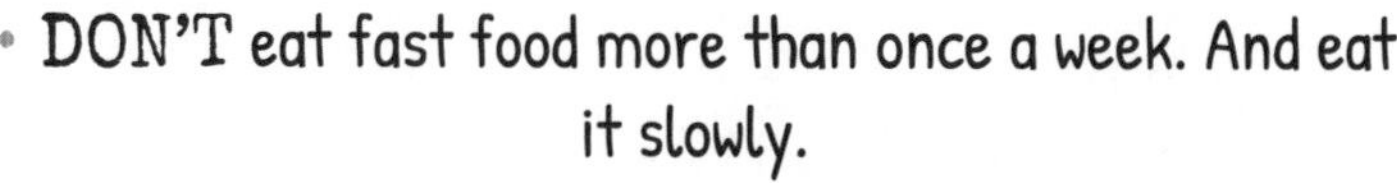

- DON'T eat fast food more than once a week. And eat it slowly.

- Plus, DON'T eat anything your great grandma would not have recognised as food.

'Slept like a log, woke up on fire'

Unknown

Guaranteed lottery win

A university study found that improving the quality of your sleep is like winning £200,000 on the lottery.

Look here, dear reader, how many times have we delivered sessions in schools and, before we even start, kids are yawning and complaining of being tired? [The answer is 'lots' btw]. So we ask them why they're tired, and guess what they say?

'I had to get up too early.'

So let's examine that sentence. Actually, you had to get up at the same time you always have to get up on a school day. It's not 'too early'. It's 'time to get up'. Therefore, the problem lies at the other end of the sleep equation, the going to bed time.

Here's some rocket science for you...

$$\begin{aligned}
\frac{1}{F(p;\xi)} &= 1 + \frac{a}{\pi p^2}\int_0^\infty dk \frac{k^2 F(k;\xi)}{k^2+M^2(k;\xi)}\left\{a(k,p)\left[-\xi\left(1-\frac{k^2+p^2}{2kp}\ln\left|\frac{k+p}{k-p}\right|\right)\right]\right.\\
&+ b(k,p)\left[2(k^2+p^2)\left(1-\frac{k^2+p^2}{2kp}\ln\left|\frac{k+p}{k-p}\right|\right)-\xi\left(k^2+p^2-\frac{(k^2-p^2)}{2kp}\ln\left|\frac{k+p}{k-p}\right|\right)\right]\\
&\left.- c(k,p)\left[2\left(1-\frac{k^2+p^2}{2kp}\ln\left|\frac{k+p}{k-p}\right|\right)-\xi\left(1-\frac{(k^2-p^2)}{2kp}\left|\frac{k+p}{k-p}\right|\right)\right]\right\}, \quad \frac{M(p;\xi)}{F(p;\xi)}\\
&= \frac{a}{\pi}\int_0^\infty dk \frac{k^2 F(k;\xi)}{k^2+M^2(k;\xi)}\left\{a(k,p)\,M(k;\xi)\left[(2+\xi)\frac{1}{kp}\ln\left|\frac{k+p}{k-p}\right|\right]\right.\\
&+ b(k,p)\,M(k;\xi)\left[\frac{2(k^2+p^2)}{kp}\ln\left|\frac{k+p}{k-p}\right|+2(\xi-2)\right]\\
&\left.+ c(k,p)\left[\frac{(2+\xi)k^2+(2-\xi)p^2}{2kp}\ln\left|\frac{k+p}{k-p}\right|+(\xi-2)\right]\right\}, \quad (15)
\end{aligned}$$

And with that cleared up, here's the opposite. If you're feeling lousy, tired and yawny, you need to go to bed earlier and/or remove the distractions from your bedroom. Phone, TV, games console – you really don't need any of those distractions (because that's exactly what they are). A bedroom is called a 'bed' room for a reason.

Your body and brain are both going through a metamorphosis, from child to teenager. It's like caterpillar to butterfly. Your body is working extra hard to regenerate, hence why you're tired. We're not wanting to nag, but it's not very clever to deprive yourself of sleep, or to be up late playing games or texting, or waking up and checking your phone. You need between 8 and 10 hours' sleep a night in your chrysalis.

Remember, your brain is growing like crazy. You're asking a lot of it. Give it a break! Night time is an opportunity for it to go to work, re-wiring, upgrading and rebooting. Give your brain and body a fair chance by getting into good sleep habits.

You want to be rich, right? You want £200 grand? Sleep well and you'll feel amazing, especially as you see the yawners sleep-walking through their non-lottery-winning lives. Oh, and when they ask you why you're always so full of energy and life, nod sagely and tell them you've won the lottery.

And that you eat lots of lettuce for breakfast.

I'm good at making decisions.

Sadly I'm not so good at always making the right ones.

[puts Fitbit in the tumble dryer and eats more donuts]

To accelerate our growth,
we must learn to fail gracefully.

Falling Flat on your Face, with Style

Your brain's number one priority is to keep you safe, hence it loves routines and habits and is not very keen on change. In fact, change can be upsetting and unsettling. The problem is that change is an inevitable element of your life. We hang on to relationships and possessions, expecting them to last forever, which they don't. Events/people/things are born, they happen, they die. Not only is that how it works, that's how it needs to work.

It's perfectly OK to have a bad time. Sometimes there's no alternative but to sit down and have a huge sob. Crying serves a purpose. It lets stuff out. It shows the world you're hurt and it's the start of the repairing process. It can be a bit messy but it's your safety valve.

If you fall down and cut your knee, it bleeds for a bit, scabs over, starts itching and eventually you spend an entire evening picking your scab off and, hey presto, good as new.

Your physical system repairs itself, and the same applies to your emotional self. All human beings come with a standard issue of 'ordinary magic', an in-built ability to heal your heart and mind.

We're not from the *Rah-Rah-Woo-Hoo* school of positivity. '*Yippee, grandma's died! What a great opportunity to have some sandwiches and cake at a funeral,*' will get you noticed for all the wrong reasons.

In a book that's about positive emotions, we think it's important to acknowledge that being sad is an important part of being happy. Think about it: a life of total joy would be bizarre. Lows are inevitable. Welcome them. Let an occasional bad day into your life, show it around, then show it the door. In the example above, a better reaction to your grandma's demise might be a heart full of sadness that lingers for a while but is replaced by pride at having had such a wonderful person in your life.

The result: you will experience grief, but be better able to move on in good time.

If you'll allow us to tell it like it is. Do you have a problem? Congratulations. Only dead people don't have problems! Happiness is not the absence of problems. It's about the ability to deal with them. Any problem is a chance to change for the better (it might be heavily disguised, but it's a gift all the same).

now + again it's inevitable

Beatriz Potter's

TRUE STORY.

Beatriz was an 8-year-old brown bear who had been trained to dance for the Russian public. She was well-travelled, secured in her 12-foot cage. Every day the keeper would let her out of her cage and she'd dance in the town square. The people would clap and throw money. Then Beatriz would climb back into her cage and they'd move to the next town.

A charity thought this was cruel so they bought the bear off her keeper and decided to release Beatriz into the wild. They took her to the forest and opened her cage door.

For the first time in her life, Beatriz stepped out into her natural habitat, the vast wilderness of the Russian mountains. She sniffed the air. Beatriz never explored. She spent the rest of her life pacing 12 feet by 12 feet.

Bea's story is both true and sad at the same time. She'd got so used to her small cage that she couldn't handle freedom. Running scared of failure means you never really go for it. A lot of people are a bit like Beatriz, living a safe but dull life. The imaginary bars you erect to protect you from the world also act as barriers that stop you fully experiencing the world. Like Beatriz, some folk spend a lifetime pacing up and down in a self-imposed mental prison cell. There is no invisible force-field.

Feel the fear

'THE greatest mistake you can make in life is to continually be afraid you will make one'

Elbert Hubbard

(Old mother Hubbard's better half. MAYBE.)

And Finally...

Earlier, we heard about Gav wanting to be a rhinoceros. Something similar happened to Andy, except not quite as bonkers. In year 6 we had a 'come to school dressed as what you want to be when you grow up' day (ctsdawywtbwygu day, as literally nobody was calling it).

Several of my mates came as astronauts. There were a couple of footballers (they were playing the 'easy costume' card), a postman, a car mechanic (no outfit as such, but he was holding a spanner) and one of the girls came as Pocahontas. I'd given my outfit a lot of thought. I knew exactly what I wanted to be when I grew up. So I borrowed some of my sister's tights, I used a towel as a cape, put my swimming goggles on and, the most important garment, I wore my pants on the outside. Yes dear reader, I went as a superhero.

Everyone had to come to the front of the class and say *why* they were dressed as they were. Pocahontas, it turned out, didn't actually want to be a native American tribal princess, she just wanted to work at DisneyLand. Eventually, it was my turn. I stood proudly in front of my class mates, straightened my goggles, hitched up my pants and, before I could speak, Mr Bell was rolling around laughing. *'What on earth are you going to be when you grow up Andrew?'* he wheezed, wiping away a tear.

I nervously hitched my pants even higher. Too high, into wedgie territory. *'I'm gonna be a superhero,'* I declared, loud and proud.

Not only did Mr Bell fall off his chair with laughter, but all the other kids joined in. My superhero chest deflated, my goggles steamed up and my pants sagged.

'There's no such job,' chuckled my teacher as I walked back to my table.

Safe to say that at age 10 it had never entered my head that you couldn't be a superhero; that there was no such job. And to this day I believe Mr Bell was totally and utterly wrong; like 110% incorrect. I firmly believe that we're all superheroes; you, me, your teacher, the lollipop lady . . . everyone. The problem is that you might have fallen into the trap of pretending to be normal.

Pants on the outside might be a step too far, but we dare you to venture into Chapter 4. It's superhero territory . . .

CHAPTER FOUR:

Your Future is So Bright You're Gonna Need SHADES

Gosh. Another big chapter that includes tombstones, superheroes and a horrible e-word. There's some bottom shuffling, growth mindset (like you've never heard it before) and some weird characters; Pants McMaths, for example.

We encourage you to get down with Mr Messy and to make a series of human sacrifices. Not literally beheading your teacher and offering her corpse to the Gods of Nimbus, oh no, something much more powerful than that.

There's some huggy stuff too, which we know you're gonna adore.

But the chapter kicks off with a wee little tale; a modern fable, no less. Cross your legs. Sitting comfortably? Then we'll begin...

The BEST jobby in the world

Have you ever tried to write a book, and not any old book, but an 'edu-tainment' one? Educating is one thing, but entertaining at the same time? It means that some bits have got boring old education in that you have to try and make funny, and some bits are just plain hilarious and you have to somehow try and shoehorn some education into them.

You probably haven't a clue what we're on about. Here's an example of where Gav had written something so ridiculously funny (and stupid) that we had to include it, and then make a lame attempt at justifying it as something deep and meaningful. Which, of course, it isn't.

SWEETCORN

A well-known fable [please choose this as tonight's bedtime story for your little brother or sister].

Once upon a time in a town far, far away, there lived a young boy. Let's call him 'Bob'. One morning Bob's mother was baking a cake for the village fair.

'Mother, Mother,' the young boy called from the top of the stairs.

Mother couldn't hear for the sound of her whisking.

'Mother, Mother,' the boy called out once again, this time running down the stairs.

Still Mother heard nothing.

Bob ran into the kitchen, *'Mother, Mother, come quick'*. Mother stopped whisking and turned with a startle. *'What's wrong young Bob? You're all of a fluster.'*

'You must come now Mother, it's important.'

The boy grabbed his mother's hand and began running towards the stairs. Mother was trying hard not to get flour all over the house. *'This had better be important!'* exclaimed Mother.

'It is Mother, it is!' replied her son.

They ran all the way up the stairs, the boy's energy

rising as they went.

'Just what is going on?' cried Mother.

'Just wait and see Mother, this is simply marvellous!'

They ran all the way along the upstairs hallway and the boy threw open the bathroom door.

'What is it?' asked Mother, wide-eyed and curious.

'It's truly one of the most marvellous things I have ever seen,' replied her son, pointing directly into the toilet. *'Look Mother, look how much sweetcorn is in my jobby.'* (Jobby is a Scottish word. It's the very best word for poop.)

The end.

Like all good fables, there is always an important message. In fact, usually three. In the case of the sweetcorn fable, stay excited, notice the little things and take pride in all that you produce.

Always.

Spotted on a tombstone:

He spent much of his life sitting on the toilet – and that was one of the best parts.

Who are you being while you're doing what you're doing?

We're avoiding the lame questions that adults ask you. *'What do you want to be when you grow up?'* Most grown-ups can't actually answer that question, so we're not expecting you to come up with a blinding flash of inspiration. Sure, you might have a dream (footballer, singer) or an ambition (scientist, doctor, vet) or some sort of notion that you want to be a nail technician or bus driver.

We're interested in a question that's more searching. Not 'what' but '*who* do you want to be when you grow up?' Not literally, as in, I want to be Martin Luther King or Henry VIII, but as in *what kind of person* do you want to be when you grow up?

There's a ninja level of goal setting and it's this: don't set a goal to achieve a goal. Set a goal so you can be the person you need to be to achieve that goal. Read it again, *sloooowly*. Is it true, or is it true?

We hang around in the adult world and, let's be blunt, most people live well within their limits. There seems little point in living your life behaving below your optimum. It's like driving a Lamborghini at 27mph. Or worse, it's like being in possession of a whole load of superpowers that you fail to use. I mean, who would you rather be, Diana or Wonder Woman, Clark Kent or Superman?

ACTIVITY:

Write down a list of people you admire. People who've achieved things; your heroes.

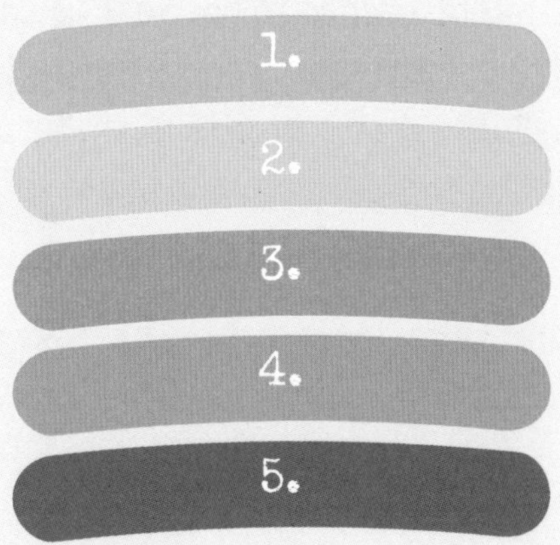

We're pretty sure your list will consist of talented people – actors, pop stars, sporting legends, that kind of thing. The modern world promotes the cult of celebrity. We are conned into thinking celebrity is something magical. It's a huge get-out clause which tells us that we're not obliged to compare ourselves with geniuses because they were born that way.

Were they? Really?

Or was there some seriously hard graft involved?

There's some smart research that says talent is important but effort counts twice. Keeping it simple, how do you become really skilful at anything? Netball, baking, painting your nails, art, gaming, building websites, pottery, tennis, maths, football, YouTubing…

Skill = Talent x Effort

When you consider individuals in identical circumstances, what each achieves depends on just two things: talent and effort. Talent relates to how fast we can improve in some sort of skill. It applies to school subjects (e.g., maths) as well as out of school (e.g., music or football). A little bit of talent is useful, but talent without effort means you'll never get skilful.

That's part one. Once you've got skilful, ask yourself what makes the breakthrough to breath-taking achievement?

Achievement = Skill x *Effort*

So hang on, effort figures again? Absolutely! Effort counts twice. You won't acquire skill without it, and you won't achieve without putting effort into honing your skills.

As Mark Spitz, multi-gold Olympic swimmer, says, 'We all love to win, but how many people love training?'

ACTIVITY:

When we were growing up, there were competitions on the back of cereal boxes. Often they were to 'complete the sentence in not more than 20 words', so, in a glorious throwback to before you were born, here's a caption to complete . . .

I am the sort of person who wants to be successful and this means that I will...

(The rules: you have 20 words or fewer and you're not allowed to use the word 'try'.)

The Succeeders

Determined dog:

The succeeders: the people who get up, dust themselves off and try again; the movers and shakers; those who can be shaken not stirred – the dogs of determination. Who are these people?

You are those people. Remember learning to walk? No? Then let us remind you. First you became really ace at shuffling on your bottom. You could really travel. Your mum would put you in the lounge and by the time she'd made a cup of tea you were away, down the street, two-cheek shuffling to Sainsbury's.

But you looked around at the adults and they didn't shuffle. Your dad did, sometimes, when he came home from the pub, but as a general rule they walked on their feet. So you thought you'd have a go. They can do it, so it can't be that difficult. You grabbed the settee and hauled yourself up. *Steady now.* And you were off. Except you weren't. Good job your botty was padded.

But you didn't sit there feeling sorry for yourself. You didn't think, *'This walking malarkey, it's not really my thing. I'm gonna shuffle on my botty till I'm 24.'*

Nope. You were determined. You wanted it badly. You failed 1000 times and then, one day, it happened. It wasn't pretty but you managed to stagger the whole length of the lounge with legs as stiff as a zombie, and, best of all, everyone applauded.

You could finally tick 'walking' off your to-do list. Next up, *how to control my bowels?*

What does this all mean? You've come a long way, baby. Also, it means that stuff that was once ridiculously hard is now relatively easy – and that's pretty much how learning works. The more you do it, the better you get. It's just that as soon as we've got something cracked, we quickly and conveniently forget the struggling that went before it.

In terms of riding a bike, 'not being able to do it' has most likely resulted in some painful failures. Not being able to get on. Falling off slowly. Falling off at speed. Falling off painfully. Not being able to stop. Looking backwards and falling off. You may even have fallen forward on to the cross bar, which will no doubt have made you very cross indeed.

In the same way that you can't make an omelette without breaking a few eggs, you can't ride a bike without breaking some omelettes. Sorry, we're getting confused.

You can't make an omelette while riding a bike.

Sorry, that's still not quite right.

There is, quite simply, no gain without a little pain – even if that pain is sometimes inside your head. It's useful to remember that whenever you feel like you just can't crack it – remember the word 'yet'. I can't do it… 'yet'.

It's called growth mindset. You already know that. How do we know you know? Because you go to a good school, you've got a fab teacher and someone loves you enough to buy you this book. Therefore, you'll have heard about fixed and growth mindsets. But your teacher doesn't always explain where the terms come from, so let's do a bit of digging into the work of the person who invented 'growth mindsets'. Let's call her Cynthia (because her actual name is Carol) – she took a bunch of kids who believed talent was born into them and compared them with kids who believed talent was achieved through blood, sweat, tears and downright effort.

Both groups were given some tough puzzles. When we say 'tough', we mean that Cynthia had designed some of the puzzles to be near impossible. Imagine if your teacher gave you a test that adults couldn't even do. That's pretty harsh.

The fixed-mindset group (the ones who thought you were either clever or you weren't, hence it was born into you or not) gave up pretty quickly, with an array of excuses along the lines of, *'I guess I'm not so smart'*, or *'I'm rubbish at puzzles'*. According to Cynthia, these clever kids simply lost faith in their cleverness.

The growth-mindset children fared differently. Remember, these kids believed that the route to success was through determination and hard work. Interestingly, when the going got tough, they kept going. They improved the quality of their strategies. A few of them even managed to solve problems that were supposedly beyond them. Crucially, they didn't focus on reasons for their failures because they didn't even consider themselves to be failing. They just hadn't figured out how to complete the puzzles. *Yet.*

The gap in performance was nothing to do with intelligence or motivation, and everything to do with mindset. Those who believed that ability was transformable through effort not only persevered but actually improved in the teeth of difficulties. Those who believed intelligence was something you either had or hadn't, well they gave up very quickly.

Fixed or Growth Mindset?

"I've missed more than 9000 shots. I've lost almost 300 games. 26 times I've been entrusted to take the winning game shot, and missed. That is why I Succeed."

Michael Jordan

(Probably the best basketball player on the planet, ever. Read that quote again. What a complete failure and also an excellent example of a growth mindset.)

Think of life as having two paths: one leading to averageness, the other to awesomeness. The averageness path is flat and straight. It's easy-peasy. You will arrive at averageness fresh as a daisy, with time to spare. But the journey is boring and the destination's a bit dull and grey.

The path to awesomeness couldn't be more different. It's steep and winding. It's longer too, requiring lung-busting effort. It's a terribly frustrating journey – it's likely you'll fall and have to start again! Just like a video game – but you only get ONE life! It's one heck of a road, but when you arrive at 'awesomeness' it's like a full-colour epic DisneyLand with fireworks and unicorns (yes, actual rainbow-coloured ones); you get to drive a hover car and eat strawberries that explode in your mouth.

A growth mindset is suited to this harder road. What we're trying to say is, yes, there's effort involved, but crikey it's worthwhile in the long run.

Narnia Thinking

Sticking with the theme, by the age of 18 most people's bodies have stopped growing, with the exception of a few nooks and crannies (check out your grandad's nose and ears). Brains, however, are different: they continue to develop – or 'grow' – throughout the course of our lives. They might not be getting any bigger (otherwise they'd be spilling out of your ears, right?) but they do 'evolve' – like Minecraft; expanding without actually getting any bigger on the outside.

So what's the big deal?

A large proportion of us, children and adults, unwittingly behave as though the opposite is true; that our minds stopped developing years ago and are limited – or 'fixed'. Or, to put it another way, some departments of our head simply get full up, meaning there's no room left for learning something new.

For instance, someone you know (it may even be you) will hold the firm belief that they're pants at maths.

It might take a while to grasp ideas introduced in class, and the whole slippery subject will most probably feel like a bit of a numbery struggle. In fact, they're probably starting to feel allergic to maths, and start sneezing and wheezing at the very thought of a rectangle. The trouble is, there's no blue inhaler for maths – try sucking up a top-heavy fraction and it gets well and truly lodged. By contrast, some of your friends (and, annoyingly, maybe even your younger brother or sister) seem to make it look easy.

All in all, that someone-you-know (Pants McMaths) has reached the conclusion that the part of their brain that deals with the number stuff is simply not big enough for the job. They've got a maths matchbox in their head, whereas others have a walk-in wardrobe.

But if Pants was better at maths, he'd probably enjoy it a bit more – and the same can be said for lots of other things in life. Unfortunately, this fixed 'matchbox maths', thinking makes it feel harder than it is.

Imagine you were running to catch a bus; if you thought there was no chance of catching it, you probably wouldn't try too hard. Why would you waste your energy on a lost cause? Because Pants believes he doesn't have the headspace for long division, he doesn't give it his all – or even anywhere close. As you can appreciate, he stands even less chance of grasping tricky concepts if he's not really bothering.

Pants is right in once respect, however: there is a part of the brain that specialises in numbers. But it doesn't look like a matchbox – or even a walk-in wardrobe. It's more like a room without any walls; it can expand to encompass, well… pretty much anything. Your very own neural Narnia. With a growth mindset, Pants McMaths would realise his brain is plenty big enough for the job. That alone should make long division easier to understand, in the same way that you're more likely to make the effort to catch the bus if you believe it's within reach.

Narnia thinking won't suddenly make Pants a long-division genius, but it could well happen eventually, if he works hard that is.

In contrast, maths comes easy-peasy to Pants' younger brother, err… let's call him Lemon Squeezy. He regularly achieves high scores in tests, and crunches numbers for fun over breakfast with his Cheerios. But even Squeezy would benefit from a growth mindset. The trouble with a fixed mindset – even one that has a high opinion of itself – is that it reaches overload at some point. (Put simply, no matter how good you are, maths will eventually become really difficult). A growth mindset would enable young Squeezy to overcome any difficulties that arise, but fixed-mindset thinking might well put him off maths (and his Cheerios). Forever. Heavy door slam.

And don't think this is just about learning maths. Fixed thinking can apply to anything you think you're good or bad at. Plus anything else you can think of. And anything else you can't think of!

A note of caution: Well-meaning friends, family, domestic pets and teachers may accidentally try and spread their fixed-mindset thinking without even realising it. Pants and Squeezy's dad, for instance, didn't enjoy maths however-many eons ago, and perhaps didn't do as well as he could've because of that.

When he heard Pants was pants at maths, he suggested it was likely to be a family trait – like having grey-blue eyes and big feet, for instance. The sort of thing that can't be helped. Unlike the colour of your eyes or the size of your feet, however, your ability to learn isn't just decided by your parents – it's decided by you.

A fixed mindset is just an excuse. After all, your dad was rubbish at art and your great great great grandma was useless at writing, so what chance do you stand?

Every chance!

That's what a growth mindset gives you.

Daydream believer

Growth mindset and effort, they're part of the success recipe. But there's something else: ambitions, goals, dreams.

The greatest obstacle to achieving your dreams is that you don't know what your dreams are.

The second obstacle is that dreams, unlike eggs, don't hatch just by sitting on them.

Everyone has hopes for the future. You might call them dreams, ambitions or goals. The things you want to make happen: successes, victories, achievements. Things that excite you.

We're offering you a blank page to draw your 'dream(s)'. The wilder the better. Think of this as the first stage of taming your wild bucking bronco of an ambition.

TRUST US. We're going somewhere with this. Get your crayons and draw what you want in life. Just one rule, you MUST get excited! Work out what your ambitions and successes are and get arty. Draw them. Create them. Protect them. Cherish them. Be them. Work hard for them. Earn them.

Most of all, colour them in (we dare you to colour in like Mr Messy, outside of the lines).

'Your future hasn't been written yet. No one's has. Your future is whatever you make it. So make it a good one.'

Doc Brown, Back to the Future

Botheredness

Let's be blunt, most people live well within their limits. Remember, there seems little point in being energised below your maximum and behaving below your optimum.

← but you're NOT 'most people'

There's a chance you may not even be aware of your superpowers. They can be heavily disguised; music, sport, writing, dance, art, history, numbers, baking, kindness, positivity, making people laugh, listening, coding, PowerPointing, acting, organising, science, YouTubing, caring, fixing, inventing, figuring things out, technology, imagineering ... any of these abilities will enable you to have a great life. But only if you discover them and bring them to life.

Delving (yet again) into deep stuff that most books don't tell you, at the core of all human behaviour, most people's needs are more or less the same. We want more positive experiences because they make us feel good and they're easy to handle. It's negative experiences that we all struggle with. But let's turn your thinking upside down – what if living an epic life isn't just about generating good feelings? What if achieving awesome things is also about being able to put up with bad feelings?

Let's explain. If I want to lose a bit of weight, I know that I will have to burn off more calories than I scoff. That's pretty much the only way it works. So, yes, I want to lose weight but not if I have to stop eating pizza, or do some, or, heaven forbid, both! So, my wanting to achieve my goal weighs less than my desire for an easy life.

Let's take another; you want to get good at playing your musical instrument. You're going to have to give something else up (e.g., less TV, less scrolling on a screen) to make massive strides forward.

The question about your ambitions and dreams is less about what you want to achieve and more like, *'What pain are you willing to sustain to achieve it'?* It's a bit weird, but what if the quality of your life is not determined by the quality of your positive experiences but your willingness to stick with negative experiences?

Think about it. Could it be that the barriers in life are put there to show how badly you want something? Or, the same meaning but worked the other way around, if the challenge we face doesn't scare us, then it's probably not that important.

That, dear reader, is a remarkably big thought. So, in the interests of challenging you, it's worth pondering what your two big goals might be, and *what you're willing to give up to achieve them.*

What am I willing to sacrifice? ACTIVITY:

We're asking you for two achievements, one at school and one outside of school (hobby, sport, music):

Big thing I want to achieve at school

What I'm willing to give up to achieve it

Big thing I want to achieve outside of school

What I'm willing to give up to achieve it

So, ear plugs at the ready, we're going to get a little shouty. **GET BOTHERED!**

Stretching yourself is good. But to maintain your motivation you need to know where you're stretching to and we're encouraging you to 'go large'. You've drawn your dream(s) so the next question is properly massive: *Where do I start?*

Getting HUGGY

Rewind. A few years ago, Andy went on a training course run by a heroic genius called David Hyner and he introduced Huge Unbelievably Great Goals.

So I got home and did one. At that time I had an idea swirling in my head about a children's book based on my pet dog. What if, while I was at work and my kids were at school, my mutt went around town catching baddies and solving crimes? What if she was a secret agent, a bit like James Bond but a dog, undercover as an ordinary family pet? What if she was a Spy Dog?

Bragging alert, but 22 titles and a million book sales later, I'm telling you, this HUGG thing really works. I've even branched out into 'Spy Cat'! I'm wondering, is 'Spy Ferret' too far?

Here's how it works. Check out the pyramid on the next page. The trick is to write your *huge unbelievably great goal* in the bubble at the top of the page, and to make it proper exciting. That means not only is it massive but that you really have to want it. It has to excite you. Whatever you draw needs summarising in one explosive sentence in the bubble at the top of the pyramid.

And when you've written it, stop and have a think. Chances are, you can write it better.

So, for example, *'To be an author'* is fine, but *'To be a best-selling author'* is finer.

'To be a vet' is nice. *'To become the best vet in my town'* is nicer.

'To get good grades' is all well and good, but *'To smash my exams so my teachers go #OMG!''* is weller and gooder.

'To get into the netball team' is stretching, whereas *'to become captain of the netball team'* is stretchier. *'To be a YouTuber'* is okay. *'To be in the world's top 10 YouTubers'* is much okayer.

You get the picture.

HUGO

nearly there

HALFWAY

NEXT step

DO every day

Get the huge goal phrased correctly and work backwards from your inspiring vision.

Start at the bottom of the pyramid and look up. What things do you have to start doing, *TODAY AND EVERY DAY*, that will move you towards your ambition? When the bottom row is filled in, you go to the next level of the pyramid. When you've started doing the things on the bottom row, what next? And next? *And after that?*

When you're finished, you will have a proper HUGG, your wild bucking bronco of an ambition, all tamed and rideable. Stick it on your bedroom wall. It will tell you what the huge goal is, and give you a simple set of things to do, or habits to adopt, that will move you forward.

There are a few more pieces to slot in, but your goal should start looking less wild. All those things in the boxes are do-able, right? But they take a bit of effort. Which is why we introduced botheredness. Life is a never-ending upward spiral. Plain and simple English yet again, that means a re-think of your thinking so that when there's a challenge, you move away from rolling your eyes and huffing that *'it's not fair'* to a steely-eyed nod of *'bring it on'*.

There are no guarantees. You will need some luck along the way. In fact, let's change the guarantees sentence – there is only *one* guarantee – your huge unbelievably great goal won't happen by accident.

It will only happen if you take action.

CHAPTER FIVE:

Bouncing Forward

Our most deadly serious chapter. Kind of.

There's lots written and said about 'mental health' and, know what? It gets us down. So we're going to flip the mental health coin. On the other side you'll find *mental wealth*, and that's what this chapter's about.

After all, you gotta get up to get down.

We've got poetry and a modern take on Humpty Dumpty and Jack & Jill. There's plenty of drawing and writing, including your happiest moments evs. Then something really important: breathing. We remind you how to breathe, cos if you forget, you die very quickly. In fact, 'not breathing' is the single biggest cause of death in the entire world.

We also have time to squeeze in some happiness concepts from around the world.

Bon appetite!

Thiiis much excited!

Gav will never forget his son's first day at school, which was, bizarrely, a Friday.

I woke up on the Monday of that week to discover 4-year-old Kian standing beside me at 6am dressed in full school uniform. I reminded him that his first day was, in fact, Friday. *'I know,'* he replied firmly. *'I'm practising.'*

He also practised Tuesday, Wednesday and Thursday, standing at the foot of my bed, ship-shape and inspection ready at 6am. On the actual Friday itself he was even earlier, fully school uniformed (jumper inside-out and shoes on the wrong feet) by 5.15am.

I smiled at my son and told him that I'd never seen him this excited before in his entire life.

'That's because I've never been this excited in my entire life.' There was a brief pause before he delivered the best bit: *'And I've been alive for four and three-quarter years!'* His eyes grew wider and he rose to his tiptoes in glee, *'In fact dad, I'll show you how excited I am. I am THIIIIS MUCH EXCITED!'*

Please picture my wee boy with his arms stretched so wide they're almost touching behind his back, shoulder blades touching. His grin was just as broad.

You can probably remember being 5. Pretty much

everything's exciting at that age, so to be beyond 'normal' excitement and to have ventured into 'THIIIS much excited', we're in 'Christmas Eve' territory.

Kian was pumped and ready for the next phase of his life. BRING. IT. ON!

So, what about you? Did you wake up this morning feeling THIIIS much excited? How often do you wake up on a Monday morning pumped, buzzing and raring to go? Are you waking up every single day energised, happy, driven and frothing with positivity? We're not talking about some days or most days, we mean EVERY SINGLE DAY!

If your answer is 'No' then there's a word for people like you: Normal.

It's absolutely normal. It's normal not to wake up every day genuinely pumped full of energy, buzzing, raring to go.

Think about this for a moment.

It's normal. You're normal.

So let's chuck a couple of questions at you. What good is having a belly if there's no fire in it?

And secondly, if 'normal' is the same as 'average', do you want 'normal'?

We're willing to put money on it that every single person reading this book absolutely categorically does NOT want normal. We bet that you are, in fact, looking for, working for, hoping for, striving for, dreaming about something absolutely extraordinary. Something exciting, purposeful, colourful and even a little bit scary. Something that makes a difference to your life and the lives of others.

Something that makes you feel THIIIS much excited.

The trick to staying excited is to wake up from your dream. There are a lot of people sleep-walking through life, not fully awake to its immense beauty. It's a gradual process – we become accustomed to our world. It becomes normal. What used to be amazing stops being amazing. We tune out. We walk past the flowers, the bright leaves, the fresh green grass, the honey-like sunlight, the frosty cobwebs and don't even notice that they're there.

We become used to them; we stop noticing how wonderful everything is and then sleep-walk through life, zombie-fied.

I'm not criticising any of us – we all do it, and it's natural.

We have been given a powerful gift – it's called 'being alive'. Here are some lists that will help you de-zombie-fy.

First of all, we want you to write a list of 50 things that you're lucky to have in your life, but that you take for granted. Yes, 50! There might be people on there, and your health, but also a bunch of little things that you forget to appreciate (like custard):

50 epic things in my life

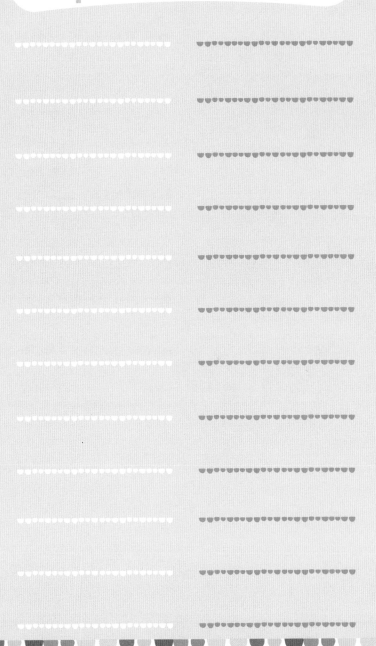

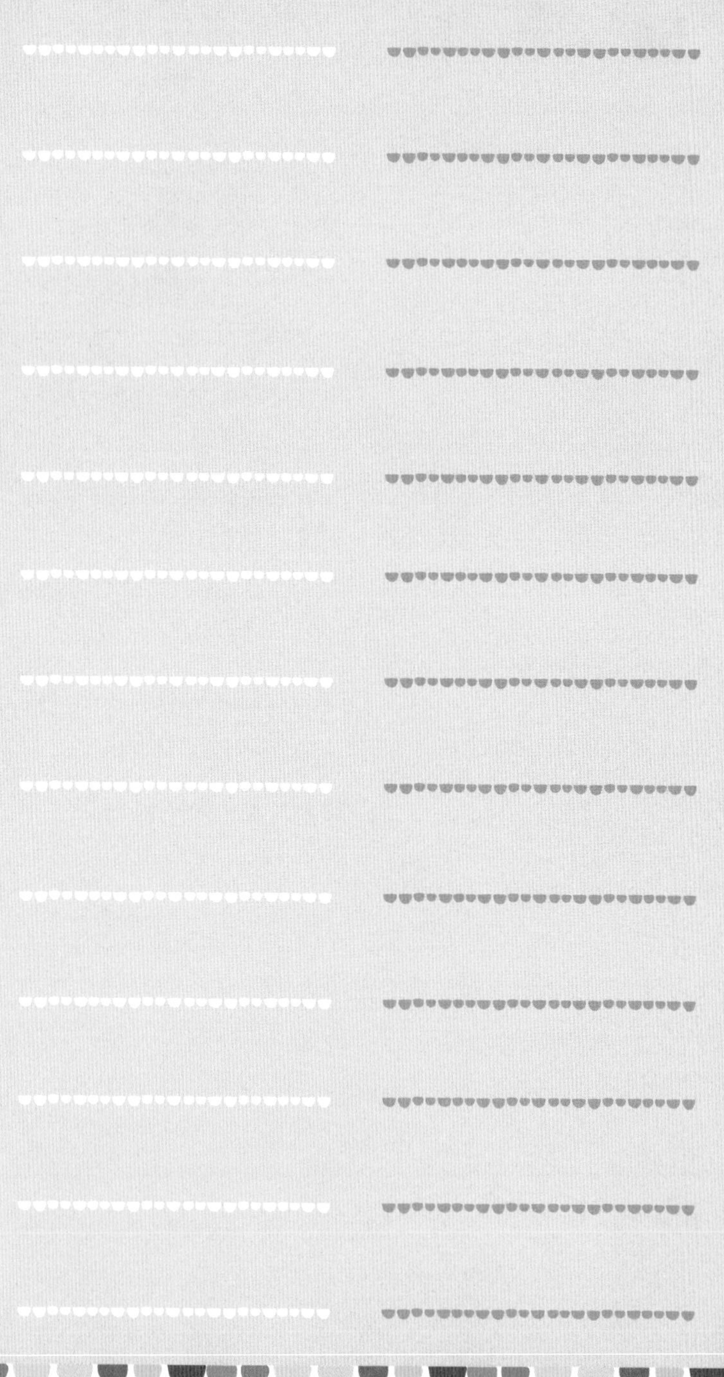

If we were going to guess what was on your list, we'd say that family, pets and 'being alive' would be near the top. Maybe having a great school and brilliant teacher. And some weird stuff crept into your top 50: flying in a plane, electricity, Wi-Fi, chocolate, soft loo roll, Cornish pasties, hot water bottles, rain, socks, toothpaste, hash browns, the ability to see and hear, oxygen, cows . . .

Most people spend a massive amount of time grumbling about what they *haven't* got. Positive people spend more time being grateful for what they *have* got. So keep the list by your bed and look at it every single day. Before your feet slip into your slippers, remember how lucky you really are.

List number 2 is harder, so we've narrowed it down to 10.

We want you to write down the 10 happiest moments of your life. Hopefully you've had millions, but we want the very best 10 moments when you felt full of joy, wonder, love and happiness. Scribble them below . . .

1

2

3

4

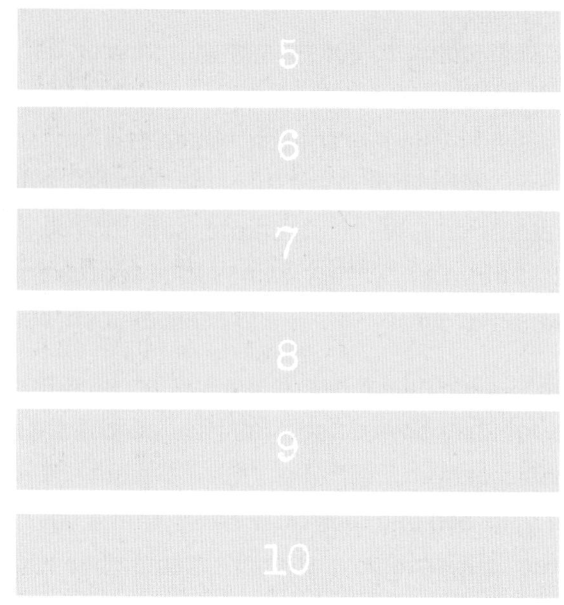

Told you this list was harder! You've had loads of happiness in your life, but narrowing it down to 10 best moments is tricky. The chances are that your 10 will be moments spent with family or friends; possibly camping, or on a school trip, or at the beach, or at a family barbeque, or Christmas Eve just gone. Or sledging in the fresh snow and then coming in and sitting your bum on the warm radiator while someone makes you a hot choc.

Your 10 moments will be 'experiences' rather than 'products'. So putting this thought out there, what if the key to happiness is not to buy more stuff from the shops, but to invest in having more experiences? Doing more things with the people you love.

Yeah. That.

Humpty re-told

Humpty Dumpty sat on a wall
Humpty Dumpty had a great fall
All the King's horses and all the King's men

Were like, 'Oh, that's so gross.
All his guts have fallen out'

Nothing but the Truth

There's a plain and simple truth that will cut out 95% of your low-level grumbling.

The world's not fair. Life's not fair. In fact, nobody ever said it was.

Expecting the world to treat you fairly because you're a fabulous person is like expecting the bull not to charge because you're a vegetarian. The bull ain't going to stop, give you a sniff and announce to the stampeding herd, *'Leave her be, lads. She's got a whiff of vegan. She means us no harm.'*

Nope, the bulls are going to keep chargin'. The news is gonna keep depressin'. The homework's gonna keep comin'. The teachers are gonna keep naggin'. The clouds are gonna keep rainin'. Your favourite team's gonna keep losin'. The haters are going to keep hatin'.

And it's totally unfair; all of it.

So grumbling that life's not fair is, quite frankly, a waste of energy and breath. Understanding that life's not fair is a decent starting point. If you're not expecting it to be fair, then you're better able to deal with bad stuff when it happens.

You've heard of 'bouncing back' after a setback. Well, how about bouncing forward? On reflection, bad stuff might not be so bad if learning from adversity means you come back even stronger than before.

Easy? No. Do-able? Yep. In fact, all the most amazing people have done exactly that.

AMY'S fave time

DOODLE time

Draw what's happened in your life so far. No right or wrong, just go for it. Let's call it, 'stuff that's made me who I am...'

Explain yours to your chum and let them explain theirs to you. Soak it up. Look at the bad stuff and explain how some good might have come out of it. What's it taught you about yourself?

And another. This time, draw how you'd like your next year to be. Think of it like a new year's revolution (yes, REVOLUTION).

As before, explain your picture to your friend. Be enthusiastic about the next 12 months. Ask yourself, what kind of habits have I got to get into to make this stuff happen? What kind of person do I have to be? What things do I have to do every single day to stand any chance of having the best year of my life?

The next step is obvious.

Do it!

Reality Bites

Here's something you're probably not expecting from a book about happiness and positivity. You need to get comfortable with *not* being okay. It's perfectly fine to feel lousy, sad, upset, bored and annoyed. Those feelings are normal and nothing to be afraid of.

Because – BREAKING NEWS – happy people feel those emotions too. Think about it. Do you expect ever to be 100% perfectly physically healthy?

Even those of you who exercise regularly and eat well probably have a few niggling aches, pains, flu, a runny snoz, poorly tummy, a verruca, sore throat or bad farts. If our physical health and wellbeing is not 100% perfect, we aren't surprised or disappointed with ourselves.

If you're still with me, then let me pose another simple question...

... do you expect to be 100% mentally perfect every moment of every day?

Of course not. Bad days are inevitable. Feeling low is perfectly okay. So is feeling stressed, sad, angry, fragile, vulnerable, lonely, grouchy and irritable. Many of us expect to lose at least a few days, if not a week or so, each year to the flu. Why don't we just expect that, at some time during the year, we might well need to have a down day?

The trick is not to feel them too often. Welcome a bit of gloom, allow it in, have a wallow if you feel the need, then show it the door. Actually walk gloom to the door, shake its hand and watch it walk away.

The big question is how? How can we move on from a bad moment or an awful day?

A harsh fact of life is that bad things do happen to good people.

I've learned, when hit by loss, to ask the right question: '*What's next?*' instead of '*Why me?*' It stops me feeling sorry for myself and helps me move forward.

I've also learned that the old adage about sticks and stones is wrong. It should read thus:

Sticks and stones can break my bones but words can permanently damage me.

Criticism and harsh words can really sting. And there are plenty of people who stand on the edges of life, throwing negativity around. Social media makes this ever so easy. Of course, you're probably too young to be on social media, right?

THE FIRST RULE is not to become one of the trolls and mud-slingers. If you haven't got anything nice to say, then keep quiet.

THE SECOND RULE is to rise above it when it happens to you. Which it will. The trick is to ignore the criticism, unless it's delivered by someone you truly respect and care for, and who cares for you too. In which case the criticism will be well intended.

From now on, the only criticism that you will accept is that delivered by those you respect and/or those whose opinion you value. Think about that inner circle of people – there won't be many. You should be able to write their names in the postage-stamp-sized box.

People whose opinions I genuinely value...

Next time someone says something bad, cruel or upsetting, check if their name is in the box. If not, you can ignore the comment because their opinion doesn't count. If their name is in the box, act on their words. They care about you, so take measures to improve yourself.

Our final words on 'relationships' and 'other people' are, we think, very powerful.

First, when you're up, your friends know who you are. When you're down, you know who your friends are. That's how it works.

And just because one person doesn't seem to care for you, doesn't mean you should forget about everyone else who does.

POETRY CORNER:

The road to wisdom?
– Well, it's plain and simple to express:

Err
and err
and err again,
but less
and less
and less
and less.

Piet Hein

WIZARDRY

You possess what's called 'ordinary magic'. It's not exactly Lumos or Alohomora, but something almost as powerful – it's your in-built ability to be super-resilient. This isn't for those trivial *'dog turd on the pavement of life'* moments, this is for when you've fallen into a barrel of the stinky stuff. So brace yourself; take a deep breath. There's going to be a terrible stench...

Someone you love will die (this will happen several times in your life), or your mum and dad will split up, or you'll get proper poorly. These are genuinely big events and they'll challenge you like never before.

Back to the dog turd thing; sometimes, no matter how positive you are, you're going to step in something rather nasty.

Ordinary magic isn't about instructing yourself to be positive or pretending the negative isn't there. It's about allowing yourself to be upset, and bouncing back stronger. We all possess this magic, otherwise known as 'time'. Time magically changes things ... eventually.

It can help if you re-train your mind to notice good things and focus your attention on them. So, notice that the sun is rising, this brekky cereal is yummy when it's gone a bit soggy, I'm breathing, my kidneys are working, look at the way the raindrops are running down the window pane, I'm in a supermarket (what an astounding choice of food), I have eyes, isn't it amazing to live in a society where bin men and women turn up and take our rubbish away, my skin is waterproof, I can read and write, I turn my cooker on and gas arrives all the way from near Denmark (how the heck did that happen?), my teacher cares about me, I have a pencil, when I turn a tap on clean water comes out.

We have an admission; almost an apology. In Chapter 4 we talked a lot about goals and growth mindset and effort. The message was that positive folk keep trying. They have resilience. They don't give up.

That's not entirely true. It works as a general rule of life, but actually 'giving up' is sometimes okay. If you've tried and tried and tried, and varied your tactics, and things still aren't working out, then giving up and moving on to something else is probably a good strategy. Maybe it's not called 'giving up'. It's 'moving on'.

It happens in friendships (the friends you have now might not be the same as the ones you have by the end of year 11), jobs and hobbies. Moving on doesn't mean you're weak, sometimes it means you are strong enough and smart enough to let go.

Oh, and one more thing: *not* getting what you want is sometimes a wonderful stroke of luck.

Jack and Jill went up the hill
To fetch a pail of water
Jack fell down
And Jill wet herself laughing
She shared the picture on Instagram
And got 600 likes

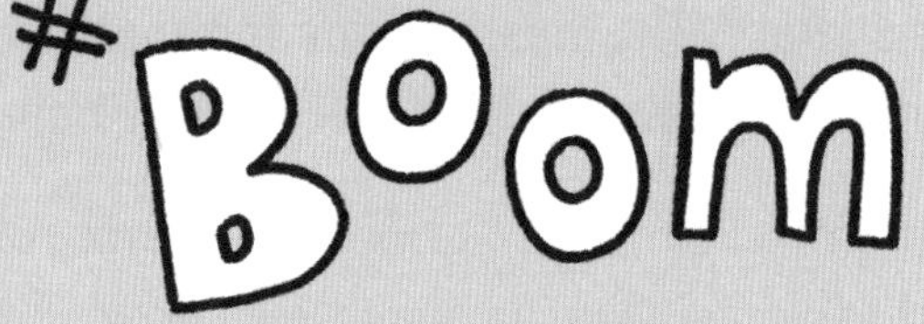

DEADLY news

Our research has uncovered an amazing statistic; something the media fails to report. The biggest killer in the UK, bigger than road accidents, cancer, heart attacks, falling off ladders and tripping over squirrels put together: '*Not breathing.*' It's literally the number one killer in the UK and the biggest cause of death across the world. It's a scandal. Yet the media fails to report it.

So breathe. And keep breathing. It's quite important.

If it's so important, maybe we should spend a paragraph on it.

Our advice: Spend 3 minutes breathing well, five times a day.

Here's how. Sit with feet on ground and straight back. Wear a small smile (and your clothes, obviously. Meditating while naked still works, but it's embarrassing if your mum comes in). Close your eyes. Breathe in through your nose for 5 seconds, hold it for 6 seconds and out through your mouth for 7.

Easy enough to remember: 5 in, 6 hold, 7 out.

Here's another. It's quick and easy, just three breaths long. Make them good breaths.

Big breath in.

First, breathe out while you consider how you feel right

now.

Big breath in again.

Second out-breath is gratitude; what have you got to be grateful for right now?

Big breath in again.

And your third breath out is what state do you want to be in? Consider and choose an attitude that will work for you going forward.

BOOM! You're back in the game.

International HAPPINESS

We think you should be a role model of happiness and positivity. That means living by the principles in this book, but also educating others. This chapter is about mental WEALTH, how to feel amazing, so here are some concepts from far-away lands.

Learn them. Do them. Show and tell them.

Shinrin-yoku, aka 'forest bathing' gives you another clue about wellbeing. The Japanese are big believers in forest bathing as a way of healing and, indeed, stopping you getting poorly in the first place. It's the simplest and cheapest remedy ever – being outdoors, in nature is good for your health and happiness. Top tip from Japan, stick your coat on and get some fresh air.

Or 'friluftsliv', which literally means 'free air life' in Norwegian, and is used often to describe a way of life that is spent exploring and appreciating nature. Similar to 'forest bathing', fresh air, nature, outdoors, jumping in puddles, hide & seek, wandering, playing, building dens… they're free medicine. The Japanese and the Norwegians, they can't both be wrong.

Halfway across the Pacific is Hawaii, with its fabulous concept of Ho'oponopono. (it's one of those words you have to say aloud, just to check how it actually sounds. Go on, if you're reading this in class, say *'Ho'oponopono'* to the person next to you). This cool word has a super-cool meaning. The Hawaiians have clicked that anger and resentment hurt the person that feels those emotions more than the one who caused them. Think about it. Anger, grumpiness, a grudge… it's like carrying a hand grenade that's stuck to you. It keeps blowing up in your face. Literally meaning 'to make right', the double use of the word pono – 'right' – indicates that you must make things right with yourself as well as the other person. Forgiveness is for your own sake as well as theirs. So, top tip from Hawaii – get over yourself!

Gemütlichkeit refers to a feeling of cosiness, contentedness, comfort and relaxation. It's difficult to say because it's German and equally tricky to translate using one word because it refers to a specific kind of feeling and situation that the words 'cosy' and 'comfortable' are too simple for. For example: A soft chair in a coffee shop might be considered 'cosy'. But sit in that chair surrounded by close friends and a hot choc, while funky music plays in the background, and that's gemütlichkeit. The Danish also have a word for it – *'Pastries'*. So, top tip from Germany and Denmark, snuggle up with a baked product.

Let's nip across to Sweden (there's actually a bridge from Denmark to Sweden, so it's easy) and introduce you to 'lagom'. Sweden is one of the happiest countries on the planet. Maybe it's because they have six months of summer when the sun never sets, or it could be their liking for naked saunas. Weird, right? 'Lagom' hasn't got a direct English translation. The best we can give you is 'enoughness'.

We know what you're thinking: so what?

Here's how the world works. Big companies spend billions on marketing, so they produce lush adverts and glossy posters that make you drool over their products. The adverts on TV are actually designed to make you unhappy with what you currently own. You might just want to read that again to let it sink in. The advert somehow convinces you that you have to buy their product to be happy. So you do, and you are. For a day or two. And then you see someone with a better phone, tablet, shoes, jeans than you, and the whole con starts again.

Purchasing things to make you happy is like putting an Elastoplast on a severed leg – long term, it ain't gonna fix the problem. There's going to be a lot of screaming and a lot of gushing.

Back to lagom – 'enoughness'; learning to be satisfied with what you already have is a pretty cool happiness trick. The world is a bit like Christmas din-dins, with everything spread out before you. Let me guess, you keep eating till it hurts? Lagom is less about knowing where to start, and more about knowing when to stop.

Please note, we're not saying 'stuff' is bad, or that money is the root of all evil. Stuff is great. And money is lush. Stuff and money won't make you unhappy, *but the relentless pursuit of more will.* Please note, this is a very grown-up point that most grown-ups don't get. Look around you and you'll see squillions of people traipsing through life in the relentless pursuit of more. Bored people binging on Netflix, fat folk stuffing their faces at Domino's, teenagers chasing a phone upgrade. *More, more, more!* If you don't believe me, poke your head into your mum's wardrobe and count the number of pairs of shoes. Ask, 'Mum, why do you have 53 pairs of shoes and 18 handbags?' and see what she says.

Then explain lagom to her.

One more: Sisu, from Finland. It's used to describe that extra energy reserve that you somehow manage to find when you're running on empty. It's that last lesson on a Friday afternoon when you find your Sisu. It's the emergency positivity that you didn't know you had. And if you combine everything in this chapter, it's what we've been pointing at all along.

The very best version of you will find your Sisu. You know it's there and are able to call on it when needed. Some circumstances are uncontrollable, but we can always decide how we react to those circumstances.

When the going gets tough, which it will, Sisu kicks in and you power ahead.

CHAPTER SIX:

Seven Little Words

'Epic' is one of those over-used words in the same way that 'flannel' is very much under-used.

But 'epic' doesn't quite do justice to our final instalment. It's whatever is just beyond 'epic'.

We're not into long goodbyes. So our last segment is a short one; short but epic. It contains the offer of a lifetime and a game of go-compare; you versus a hummingbird. Weird!

What could possibly follow an offer and a game? A mind-blowing experiment, obviously. Prepare yourself for 20 minutes that will change your life. Then it's onto eyelashes, brain-twisters and we've only gone and done what Andy does at mealtimes: saved the best bit till last.

You'll notice quite a few NOWs btw. Oh, and we finish with seven words that will change your life. They're not quite what you expect but, hey, if you've got this far, you've come to expect the unexpected.

Thanks for hanging in there. We're delighted you've reached this point. Proud, in fact. Of you, not us!

Couldn't be prouder.

Thank you.

TOP TIP:

Cut down massively on TV, YouTube, X-Box, PS and Social Media. We're not saying cut it out completely. But les is better. While everyone is X-Boxing the life away you can be getting on wi

Secret long-term ambition

That's what we did and it WORKED!

The Experiment

Wouldn't it be a shame to have a wonderful life and not notice?

A lot of people do. Have a wonderful life, that is, and not notice. They grumble about their wonderful life instead.

Challenge

Here's a challenge, and an experiment: a ch-eriment. Twenty minutes that might change your life. It's probably something you're going to have to ask your teacher to help you with. Maybe the whole class can take part. It takes exactly 20 minutes and for the first 10 your teacher is going to really suffer (hence, please explain that you're doing a ch-eriment, a world first, as stated in this best-selling, award-winning book. Stick the page under your teacher's nose and tap the page knowingly).

For the next 10 minutes, sit and behave negatively. Have a stinking attitude. Don't be bothered about happiness, positivity or effort. Slump in your chair. Stick a sullen look on your chops. Do some huffing and maybe some puffing. Fold your arms. Tut whenever someone suggests something. Whatever your teacher does, imagine it's Dullsville USA, the dullest town in all of the Dull-iverse. Imagine the world is against you and everything, even the weather, is unfair.[9]

[9] If you find this 10 mins is just how you normally are, then the problem's bigger than we thought.

[Sorry teacher!] 10 minutes. Got it? *Go!*

How did it feel? How long did those 10 minutes feel? How's your energy? How did your learning go?

Now the opposite. For the next 10 minutes, sit and behave like one of the 2%ers we mentioned in Chapter 1 – a positive version of you. Don't be ridiculously over the top, but we want you to choose a great attitude. Get bothered. Smile. Work hard. Sit upright in your chair. Put your best face on. Stick your hand up and try, even if you're not sure of the answer. Be gripped by whatever the subject is. Imagine this lesson is an opportunity for you to learn and grow and expand your mind. Be properly interested. Imagine the world is amazing and everything, even the weather (even if it's raining) is brilliant.

10 minutes. Got it? *Go!*

How did it feel? How long did those 10 minutes feel? How's your energy?

If you experimented properly, the first 10 will have felt like an eternity and you learned nothing. It was a drag. It was a waste of 10 valuable minutes of your young life. The second 10? You'll have felt different. It zipped by, you enjoyed it, you were engaged and, guess what, your teacher loved it.

Our experiment only lasted 20 minutes but you will have noticed a big difference in how you and your teacher feel. The message? If you've got this far into the book we reckon you can work it out for yourself. Was it really just about those 20 minutes, or was it about something much bigger?

Choices, dear reader, choices. You get to choose your flavour of life. It's blinkin' obvious.

Which brings us onto eyelashes. Wherever you are, put this book down for a few seconds (yes, I know it's so good it's un-putdownable, but trust us) and take a look around.

Look up, down, left, right, roll your eyes around, and what do you see?

Lots, probably. But not your eyelashes, that's for sure. They're everywhere you look, but you never see them.

Choosing a positive attitude is the same. Or at least its potential is.

It's so obvious that we miss it. The choice to be positive is with you in every moment, everywhere you tread, the ultimate portable super-power, and yet almost nobody uses it.

Interestingly, the attitude choice thing doesn't work the other way. Nobody chooses to be miserable, grumpy or angry. Nobody slumps out of bed thinking, 'I'm determined to have a real stinker today' (I appreciate that it might seem that way, but I promise you it isn't).

Most people just get out of bed, often a bit tired and

grumpy because it's too early.

Reflect back on first thing this morning. Did you rise and shine, or rise and whine?

Exactly!

The 'rise and whine' thing. It's a very easy habit to get into, hence why nearly everyone does. But you're not 'everyone'. You're you. You're going to be extinct in the next 90 years. You're the last one of your kind left in the wild. You owe it to your species to be at least a little bit lively, interested and positive.

Sounds obvious. But it isn't. For almost everyone, 'the day' decides how they feel. On a good day, when the sun is shining and things are going well, the conditions are right for you to be happy and, guess what, you are! Yippee! Until the sun goes in, or you get stuck in maths, or Aimee doesn't invite you to her party, or you get picked last at football.

Most people are waiting for the world to be right first, and when those conditions are met, then they'll be happy. But if you're waiting for the perfect happiness conditions, you'll be waiting an awfully long time!

In fact, you'll become extinct waiting. The choice to be positive comes from inside. It's entirely in your head. It's something you need to do NOW. And NOW. And NOW. For all your NOWs.

Forever.

And ever.

Brain-twisters

Here are a few things to ponder. On a wet Wednesday afternoon when top-heavy fractions are dragging on a bit, ask your teacher if you can throw these brain-twisters into the mix:

Class discussion #1: If you do what's easy, your life will be hard and if you do what's hard, your life will be easy. True or false? Explain.

Class discussion #2: People who live in comfort zones are actually extremely uncomfortable. Discuss.

Class discussion #3: It's OK. It's always OK. Except when it's not and that's OK as well. Waddayathink?

Class discussion #4: Go out looking for friends and you will find very few. Go out and be a friend and you will find many. What do you and your classmates think?

Class discussion #5: Being lazy pays off now. Hard work pays off in the future. Discuss.

Class discussion #6: What 20 things would you like for Christmas ... that aren't things?

A ONCE-A-LIFE OFFER

Let's make you an offer – not just a holiday – the adventure of a lifetime!

Let's imagine, just for a moment, that we've invited you on an amazing trip into the solar system. We're going to spend the next 90 years cruising amongst the stars. In fact, let's upgrade the trip... let's go the long way and journey around the sun. The holiday is free and, in true game-show style, we'll throw in some spending money.

The big question is: would you go?

Ninety years is a long time, right? You're thinking that you'd miss your family, friends and cat. So let's upgrade you further. So you're not lonely, you can take all your family and friends, your cat/dog/guinea pig, your house and, the clincher, we'll give you Wi-Fi.

You're probably thinking there's a catch. You can't possibly be offering a lifetime of space travel, with family and friends and Wi-Fi! For FREE?

And yes, there is a catch.

Welcome to Earth. This is the journey you are already on. Your home is a ball of rock, spinning on its axis as it hurtles through space at 67,000 mph (thanks Wiki). Around us are billions of other lumps of rock. Earth travels all the way around the sun every single year. You already have friends, family and Wi-Fi; maybe even some spending money too.

Open your eyes. We really hope you're enjoying the adventure. It's the adventure of a lifetime; your lifetime.

HEART to HEART

Let's play a game. Line up a giant tortoise, a hummingbird, your favourite pet… *and you.*

What have they all got in common (apart from good looks, of course)?

The answer is that they're all born with about a billion heartbeats to spare. It's why animals with slow heartbeats live longer. So your giant tortoise goes on and on and on for 200 years and your hummingbird only has about 4 years.

An interesting question arises out of this story, and that

is: what are you going to do with your billion heartbeats?

The wise readers will figure that if they look after themselves they're likely to get more than a billion. But the message might be even bigger than that.

Last week Andy went to his grandad's funeral. It was a very sad occasion and Andy had chance to reflect on what a 'good life' actually was. His grandad had had an okay one. He was a decent bloke who'd worked hard as a bus driver. Andy decided three things. First that he wanted to die peacefully in his sleep, like his grandpa did, not screaming and yelling like his passengers. Second, he wasn't sure exactly how many heartbeats he had left, but he was going to treasure them. Every single one from now on. And third, he was going to write about his grandad and stick the story in this book.

You've used up about 100 heartbeats reading this story. Wasted? Not if it's made you think a bit and consider upgrading your life to 'epic'.

Skip to the Loo

Skip to the Loo,
Skip to the Loo,
Skip to the Loo,

Too late, anyone got a change of trousers?

All good things

Let's finish with one of Gav's lessons. Sit back, relax and enjoy.

So there I was, week 1 of Primary School, 5 years old and learning to fit in, whatever that means. It was Friday and my school experience so far had been outstanding: new friends, old friends, Hide 'n' Seek and as much sand-pit time as I could possibly imagine.

Magic.

We came back in to the class after breaktime, fresh from a game of tig. The Head Teacher, Miss Smart (real name) popped in for a chat.

'Good morning boys and girls.'

'Gooooooood mmmmoooorrnning Miiiisss Smaart.'

Miss Smart was about to tell us something that would be a game changer for me. *'Boys and girls, for the first time ever, this Christmas, we are going to put on a school pantomime.'*

I couldn't believe what I was hearing; a pantomime, in my new school. I loved pantomimes.

'Not only are we putting on a pantomime boys and girls, but we need some of you to be in it.'

Well, this just about sent me over the edge. I think

a bit of wee slipped out. My school was putting on a pantomime and some of us were going to be in it!

'We will be doing Jack and The Beanstock.' (Miss Smart is Scottish, remember.)

My absolute favourite pantomime ever. I could see in my mind the giant's enormous legs walking across the stage as *'Fee Fi Fo Fum'* rang out across the theatre.

'We need five pupils from this class to be the mice who run on stage every night and steal the giant's cheese.'

Steal the cheese! Oh. My. Goodness. I could picture it: me on stage. I was imagining myself sitting in the audience; I could see the mice, the cheese and, again, the giant's legs ... and me.

I was beyond excited.

Throughout life we are presented with opportunities. I was about to be presented with one that would ultimately shape my entire life.

'Hands up if you want to be one of the mice in the pantomime?'

My hand was up on the 'a' of 'Hands'.

'Wee Gavin Oattes.'

Yikes, had she noticed? Never mind, she picked me. This was it, this was my moment.

'Your hand was up first, do you want to be a mouse?'

All of a sudden I could picture the audience from the stage. Hundreds of people watching me. What if it went wrong? What if they didn't enjoy it? What if I wasn't good enough? What if I was pants at being a mouse?

My unbelievable excitement turned to unbelievable fear.

'Do you want to be a mouse?' Miss Smart repeated.

Again, all I could see was the audience staring back at me. All of a sudden I knew what it meant to be a worrier.

'No thanks, I only put my hand up because I need to go to the toilet.'

Everyone laughed.

My teacher stepped in...

'Are you sure Gavin, you seemed awfully excited.'

I repeated myself. *'I only put my hand up because I need to go to the toilet.'*

'OK then, on you go,' she said as I ran out the door.

I ran all the way to the toilet, ran into a cubicle, locked the door and burst into tears. I had never felt like this before. Five years old and I felt like my world had come to an end ... over a pantomime.

It might seem a little overdramatic, but to put this into a 5-year-old's perspective, it was my absolute dream to be in a pantomime. I had always wanted to be in one.

I had my chance and I blew it. Seven years of primary school passed and not once did I set foot on a stage. Not once did I volunteer for anything that involved possible public humiliation. That moment stuck with me forever. I allowed the fear to get the better of me. That day affected my confidence for a very long time. In a strange irony, I kind of turned into a mouse.

Then came high school. My dream was still to be on stage. I continued to turn down every chance I had to get up and perform; I was so worried about what others might think. Even more opportunities passed. Even reading aloud from a book in class became an issue for me. My face would turn bright red and my classmates would laugh.

FACT: When your face turns red with embarrassment, so does the lining of your stomach. Cool huh?

I was still dreaming of being on stage, performing and entertaining hundreds (maybe thousands one day) of people in a theatre. By 15 years of age I was obsessed with comedy: stand-up comedy, comedy films, TV shows, books, basically anything that was really silly and made me laugh. I would sit in my room at night writing comedy sketches, filling notebook after notebook with all the nonsense stored in my brain. Maybe one day I would get to share this nonsense with the world.

It doesn't matter who you are, where you're from or what anyone else thinks of you. You are allowed to believe in you. You are allowed to be confident in you. You are allowed to step out of your comfort zone and when you spot an opportunity that looks and feels right, grab on with two hands, keep your feet on the ground and run as fast as you possibly can.

If you don't, then one day you might just look back and wonder: what if?

At 18 years of age I finally went for it. If there was ever a job for someone terrified of crowds, public humiliation and other people's opinions, it certainly wasn't stand-up comedy.

So, naturally I became a stand-up comedian.

I did my first gig. It felt incredible. Over the last 20 years I have performed all over the world: good gigs, terrible gigs, great gigs. So many ups and downs. I've met the most wonderful people, and the main thing I have learned is this – if you're faced with an opportunity that's both terrifying and amazing then you should totally go for it.

Yeah, all of you.

Here are seven words that, if you stick to them, will change your life:

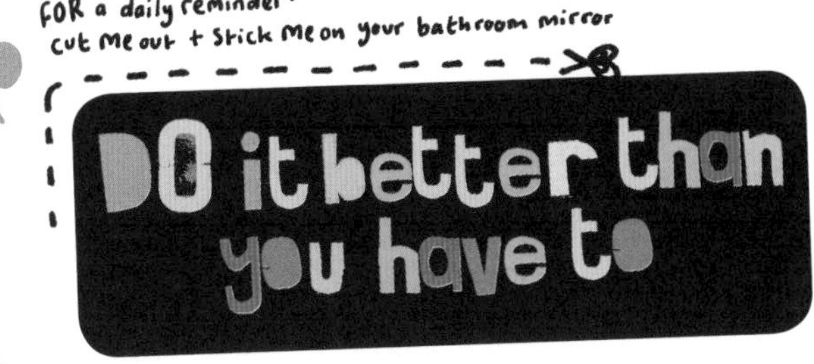

FOR a daily reminder:
cut me out + stick me on your bathroom mirror
DO it better than you have to

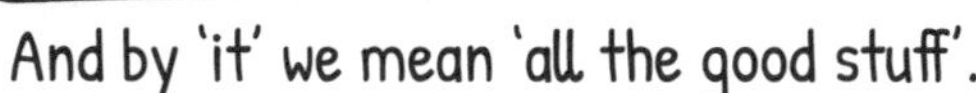

And by 'it' we mean 'all the good stuff'.

Use your manners a bit better than you have to.

Work a bit harder than you have to.

Do your homework a bit better than you have to.

Be a bit more positive about yourself than you have to.

Smile a bit more than you have to.

Eat a bit healthier than you have to.

Play a bit less on your games console than you have to.

Read a few more books than you have to.

Believe in yourself a bit more than you have to.

Get out of bed with a more positive attitude than you have to.

Respect your teachers and parents a bit more than you have to.

Help out at home a bit more than you have to.

In fact, do all these things because you want to.

And if you do, you'll stand out a mile. Because most people do what's easiest. Most people do pretty much what they have to and no more. Your little extras build and build into something special.

Making you someone special.

Here's the truest thing ever: you cannot be anything you want to be – but you can be a LOT more of who you already are.

Life's short.

Go make good things happen.

Go make good things.

Go make good.

Oh my goshness! You've only gone and completed the entire book! Remember, the principles are simple but that doesn't mean they're easy. Practice makes perfect, so we think you've earned a 'Brill Kid' certificate, not just to celebrate finishing the best book evs, but to remind you to keep practicing being your best self. There's a blank certificate waiting for you here www.artofbrilliance.co.uk so log on, fill your name in, print it off, stick it on your wall and hey presto – you're a fully-fledged 2%er

#wahooooooo!!!

er, HURRY!!!

Certificate OF AWESOMENESS
Congratulations on completing
Diary of a BRILLIANT KID
You are now a trainee superhero
Read. Learn. Do.
PS, your training never stops
pigeon flamingo
BRILL KID
yum

the AUTHORS

• ANDY COPE

Andy's got a bonkers life. He writes the world famous 'Spy Dog' stories and is also the UK's one and only Dr of Happiness. YES, that's an actual thing that you can be a doctor of! Who knew?

Dr Andy works all over the world delivering happiness and wellbeing workshops for businesses and schools. He's even been to Botswana. He's also written a shed load of teenage and adult books but you're probably not interested in that. He's got some pet pigs, is that interesting enough? He recently got badly stung by a jellyfish and had to have a bath in vinegar? That's proper interesting, right?

If you want to know more about Andy, check him out at www.artofbrilliance.co.uk, follow him on Twitter (beingbrilliant), Instagram (spydog451) or drop him an email at andy@artofbrilliance.co.uk.

• GAVIN OATTES

Part child, part rock star, Gav is one of the best and silliest humans around. He runs a properly awesome company called 'Tree of Knowledge' whose purpose is to Inspire the World. And on a daily basis – within schools and businesses – that's exactly what they do. As part of this Gav and his team have worked directly with over 1,000,000 young people, empowering them to follow their dreams and be the best, kindest humans they can be.

He regularly does crazy things such as booking huge arenas and filling them with 12,000 people for MAHOOSIVE days of inspiration and learning.

If you want to know more about Gav and find out why companies such as
NIKE book him to fire up their people, check him out at www.gavinoattes.com and/or www.treeof.com, follow him on Twitter (gavinoattes), Instagram (gavoattes), Facebook (Gavin Oattes) or drop him an email at gavin@gavinoattes.com.

WILL HUSSEY

Will's real talent is rippling his tongue; that's right – like a snake. TRY IT. It's impossible. When he was 10, Will remembers his dad writing a book, which he thought was a pretty cool thing to do (even though it had absolutely nothing to do with snakes.) And neither does this, but Diary of a Boa Constrictor probably wouldn't make much sense ...'

AMY BRADLEY

Amy is a FUN girl!

She has been drawing for as long as she can remember; it was her favourite thing to do as a kid and now, as a fully fledged adult, she reckons being an illustrator is the best job in the world!! Beat that hey!

She works out of her very own quirky studio in Uttoxeter, Staffs. Here, you'll never see her wearing shoes ... shoes totally cramp her creative style! And for when she really has to concentrate ... out comes the 'secret stash' ... chocolate, biscuits, cookies and 'Donut' worry; Donuts!! (Her all time fave!!).

Amy is super excited because she's recently received the amazing news that her illustrations will soon be hitting the big screen on Cbeebies in 'Its About Time' ... proof dreams really can come true! Eekkkk!

If you wanna know more about Ames, then check out: www.amybradley.co.uk, follow her on Twitter: @amy_brad1 or even drop her an email: mail@amybradley.co.uk

Index